FOUNDATIONS OF MUSIC EDUCATION SERIES
Allen P. Britton, Editor

Junior

High School

General Music

PRENTICE-HALL INTERNATIONAL, INC., *London*
PRENTICE-HALL OF AUSTRALIA, PTY. LTD., *Sydney*
PRENTICE-HALL OF CANADA, LTD., *Toronto*
PRENTICE-HALL OF INDIA LIMITED, *New Delhi*
PRENTICE-HALL OF JAPAN, INC., *Tokyo*

Junior
High School
General Music

FRANCES M. ANDREWS

The Pennsylvania State University

PRENTICE-HALL, INC., *Englewood Cliffs, New Jersey*

780.729
An 2j
786 5 5
May 1972

Current printing (last digit)
10 9 8 7 6 5 4 3 2 1

Library of Congress Catalog Card Number: 70-144007

Printed in the United States of America

C-13-512442-5
P-13-512434-4

Foreword

The practical aim of the Foundations of Music Education Series is to provide music educators with a unified but highly flexible and completely authoritative treatment of the most important professional concerns. Individual books of the series may be combined in various ways to form complete textbooks for the wide variety of courses in music education offered by colleges and universities across the nation. On the other hand, each volume has been designed to stand alone as a definitive treatment of its particular subject area.

The pedagogical aim of the series is to present practical and proven techniques of successful teaching in compact and readable form for both college students preparing to teach and experienced teachers constantly searching for more efficient ways of thinking and teaching. The highest musical ideals must be accompanied by the greatest amount of practical common sense if music instruction is to be most successful.

The aesthetic aim of the series is to emphasize the purely musical values that must be realized in any program of music instruction if that program is to achieve ends worthy of the time and effort required to carry it on. In short, each of these works assumes first of all that music must be true to itself if it is to continue to hold a respected place in American education. The most telling criticisms made of the school music program in recent years, almost all of which have dealt largely with alleged aesthetic failings, have written this lesson in letters large enough for all to read.

Last, having pointed out the unifying concepts that underlie the works in this series, it is perhaps equally important to emphasize that each of the authors has written the book that he wanted to write, the book that he believed would be of most value to the profession. The series encompasses the individual convictions of a great variety of the most highly competent and experienced music educators. On their behalf as well as on my own, may I express the hope that it will contribute in a practical way to the improvement of music teaching.

ALLEN P. BRITTON,
EDITOR

Preface

The intent of this book is to help teachers become more effective communicators of music. The book is dedicated to the many men and women the author has known as outstanding music educators; both "he" and "she," rather than the usual single designation, are used when referring to the teacher.

The music educators to whom this book is dedicated have an outstanding characteristic in common: a constant search for ways in which to improve their teaching.

A word with regard to the difficulty level of materials and procedures in this book: Junior high school grades have traditionally included seventh, eighth, and ninth. The range and variety of individual music experiences in and out of school, however, indicate that the teaching of music should be adapted by each teacher in such a way as to arouse and challenge the interest of boys and girls regardless of grade level constraints. If materials are too easy or too difficult the teacher should feel free to rework them. Music instruction must be adapted to particular classes and individuals to as great an extent as the teacher finds possible.

Frances M. Andrews

Contents

Junior

High School

General Music

Introduction

Were an attempt made to summarize the junior high school music problem in one sentence, it might be said that its teachers are uncertain about what it is they are to teach, and pupils about what they are to learn. No better recipe for chaos in the classroom could possibly be devised. The recipe has worked! For when pupils are not learning whatever it is they are supposed to be learning, they don't stop learning; they simply find other things to learn. A variety of matters are learned in such a situation, including negative attitudes toward singing, listening, the teacher, reading music, and a whole classification of music regarded as "square." It is true that some children *insist* on remaining interested in music, but when one examines such cases it often develops that private study, or instrumental study, have been the generating forces of the persistent interest.

The unhappy conclusion that emerges is this: The one type of music instruction required for all, or most, of our American boys and girls is the least dynamic in approach, the most depolarizing so far as holding the attention of students, and the only area in which we do not really prepare music specialists.

Teachers of music are likely to complain that young people like music

1

that is trivial and inferior. Examples of this are rock and country. Yet youngsters seem to like this type of music because it is an emotional release, an emotional pacifier, probably because on one hand it "psychs" them up, and on the other hand, it is an emotional stimulus. Both may be constituting a release. Isn't it strange that this emotional approach (mood of music) is the approach many teachers have been using, but *unsuccessfully;* in the classroom it doesn't work. Why? The pupils need something more to hold their interest in school. They insist on expecting to learn when in school.

There seems to be a dichotomy in the viewpoint of American music educators. Those who work with instrumental and choral groups appear to believe that music is for the talented few. Forty-eight years of MENC's informal slogan, "Music for Every Child and Every Child *for* Music," has done little to change their minds. A second group of music educators is every bit as devoted to the belief that music in some form *is* for *every child.* Not even they, however, have been so bold as to claim that every child *is* for *music.* Nor is there any empirical evidence to support attainment of the slogan. Between these two groups there is a somewhat ambivalent, free-swinging group who are half and half—they commit their efforts to the idea of attempting to bring some music to the life of every child, but it is not a matter of great concern if only a few children end up with a reasonable amount and quality of musical experience.

The position of the first group of teachers, the "talented only" group, is somewhat justified if we accede to the belief that not all will be, or will even wish to be, performers—in whatever sense the term may apply. Then too, it is a more or less defensible posture in terms of teacher comfort and fulfillment; there is satisfaction for the frustrated would-be performer in the performance of his pupils, who in turn receive a degree of positive encouragement bearing a particular psychological urgency. But one must work mostly with the more talented pupils to bring all of this about.

This is not to imply that the teacher-musician cannot be a first-rate performer. But it is easily perceived that such an individual can really afford to work only with the more talented, for work with the average and below-average in talent is very time-consuming, and the teacher-performer (one who is performing publicly, vocally or instrumentally) must maintain and develop his skill through extensive practice, if he is to progress professionally.

The fatal flaw in the philosophy is that it leaves a large residue of the school population unserviced—and the schools are for *all,* theoretically and philosophically. Therefore, the school curriculum is for all. The second group of teachers is willing to implement the "all" philosophy; they make a fair showing in the elementary school, although some portion of the classroom music program is often carried on by the classroom teacher. The music "supervisor," "consultant," "special subjects," "visiting" or "on-call" teacher in many schools is more often on the sidelines than in the game, possibly responsible for hundreds of classrooms monthly. Certainly some classroom teachers are interested, competent, and effective in music. But adding insult to injury in the cases of inadequate preparation, certain teacher preparation institutions require *no* music courses of their elementary education majors. It is apparent that not even the K-6 music program is what might be envisaged and achieved, even by those who believe music *is* for all.

In the junior high school, one might hope and expect that there would be more and better general music instruction, for here the teaching is in the hands of music specialists. "Hoping" is about as far as this goes, for few institutions encourage or prepare their music education majors to teach *all* the pupils in general music. Rightly or wrongly—and this author does not make a judgment here—the emphasis in the teacher music education curriculum is on *music per se* and musical performance. The latter is an alluring, exciting part of the love of music. It polarizes students who can perform even passably, and it persistently and inexorably consumes their time, rehearsal after rehearsal, performance after performance, whether center stage as a soloist or pit orchestra as second clarinet. Even for the "always-a-bridesmaid-never-a-bride" orchestra, band, or chorus members there are two magnetic poles, and *not* diametrically opposed as north and south. These are the allure of being near the star performers, and the mystical dynamism of being at once submerged and yet uplifted as part of a performing group—even a small part. Although this is at its peak under the charismatic, convergent effect of a superb conductor, the magnetic field exerts some force even under the less gifted individual when he mounts the podium for a public performance.

None of these forces, and no comparable force, acts to impel the young, would-be music educator in the direction of the general music class. If the student is a promising musician, he is strongly encouraged, even pressured, to devote his attention, his interests, his time, and his talent to performance, musicology, or composition. If he is not, but is less promising as a performer and more as a teacher, he is still a "warm body" available for performing organizations, particularly to fill up "second" groups, or even "first," if his instrument or voice is needed.

Backing up a step, the mediocre high school musician has little chance of even being accepted in a top-level school where the emphasis in interpreting criteria used to judge acceptability of future music educators is as much or more on musical achievement as on academic record or potential as a teacher. This is at once both the great strength and the weakness of our profession, for no other teacher preparation curriculum demands the degree of subject specialization that music does. And no other curriculum penalizes its future teachers to the same extent for planning or wanting to teach. The music education major is often a second-class citizen, and is too often encouraged to major in *music* but acquire the necessary certification (necessary in case he must "fall back on teaching" for a livelihood) as a strictly adjunct and auxiliary activity through completing *credits* rather than a *program*. This attitude creates ambivalence and uncertainty in those young people who wish to teach but perceive "music educator" as being a somewhat less than desirable label to carry through life. The implications of all this are that teachers of general music must be given status, self-identity, and prestige if they are to specialize to a point where the general music program is successful. It will be successful only when teachers are prepared to deal with it as a substantial and important area of the curriculum.

1

The General Music Class

DEFINITION

The general music class is the segment of the music program that includes all pupils. This is one application of the term "general"—to the total population, as well as to the content of the course. Music should be taught to pupils grouped in classes that approximate the size of other subject classes. It is a course intended to develop musical skill, knowledge, appreciation, and above all, musical judgment and discrimination that will develop the cultural and aesthetic sensitivity of the pupil—the present and future citizen.

This class is *not* a chorus, and not a group singing fest. It is a legitimate learning situation devoted to musical activity.

In the total music program each pupil deserves and has the right to:

1. The opportunity to explore and test his own abilities to make music.
2. The opportunity to develop and sensitize his potential for responding to music in many forms, styles, and periods, ranging from music of primitive man to that of the present day.
3. The opportunity to learn to understand the structure and basic elements of music from an intellectual viewpoint.

4. The opportunity to identify emotionally and aesthetically and develop empathy with music as it evokes listener response; the opportunity to *enjoy* music.

5. The opportunity to experience the making of music in such groups as choruses, bands, orchestras, and small ensembles, and to make music as an individual.

6. The opportunity to become, if adequately talented, highly skilled in the making of music as a soloist.

7. The opportunity to learn to appreciate and develop values with regard to music as a cultural heritage through knowledge of its many aspects, such as historical, sociological, and performing.

8. The opportunity to understand music as a living art, and as part of our contemporary life—what music is appropriate to what occasions and why (for example, weddings, funerals, receptions, dances, church services, commencements); how good taste in choosing and judging music is developed.

9. The opportunity to learn to attend, appreciate, and enjoy concerts—the audience experience. All artists look to the audience as a source of renewal and, to some extent, set their standards according to audience expectations. Pupils should have the opportunity to develop values with regard to, and to become at home with, the meaning of program content.

10. The opportunity to learn to play a musical instrument when the urge is the greatest, even though this may be during the junior-senior high school years. The question of what *use* an individual will be as a future member of a performing organization should be considered separately; the years fourteen through eighteen in age may be too late to begin the training of a *professional* musician, but this cannot be said to apply to an *amateur*. In considering this problem we come to grips with the "music for the good of the pupil, or music for the pupil only if he is organization talent" philosophy. It is a real test of belief with regard to the function of music in the public schools.

11. The opportunity to have the benefits of a music curriculum that makes sense in terms of reality of content, materials, procedures, and musical experiences.

Not all the above can be taught in general music classes, of course. But checking over the list may help identify what can be done in such classes that is not being accomplished in any other part of the music curriculum; careful consideration of the points listed may result in music class experiences pulling together as an integrated whole the various segments of a pupil's musical education.

DIAGNOSIS

It is probable that an unrealistic curriculum, in both content and approach, has done more to kill the general music program than any other single factor. This is too often combined with an impractical and unrealistic attitude on the part of music teachers, an acquired attitude dictating that no matter what the cultural level of the pupils concerned, only the so-called "best" music shall be used. Thus a beginning teacher going into a rural community where the chief musical exposure has been to hillbilly or country music may both by conscience and training be impelled to teach, for example, Bach, Brahms, or baroque music, a path with suicidal implications. Considering that pupils by junior high school age are fairly well conditioned to certain types of music through their radio and television experiences, it is not only useless but also cruel to begin with materials that are remote from their conditioning, even if one attempts to reconcile such material with reality.

What happens to a junior high school teacher in this situation? The obvious answer is that, not knowing how to solve the problem of stimulating and developing interest in the "best" music, or being unwilling or unable to devote the requisite amount of time to planning interesting lessons that will combine a variety of music materials, the junior high school teacher concentrates on developing performing organizations. The general music program is left to generate disinterest, disorder, and a degree of curricular malfunction.

Probably the so-called "general" music class has another disadvantage—the word "general." General music would be better entitled simply "music." The content has its general aspects, as does any subject taught in the schools, but it also has, or should have, specific aspects. For some reason the term "general" implies matters dull and boring, while "specific" implies sharp, interesting focus. The general portion of the music class should be that which develops pupils' understanding of music through basic conceptual understanding of the elements of pitch, duration, timbre, loudness, and form, the organizational structure of music. These involve all musical experiences. The specific aspects of the music class should concern the way composers and performers use these musical factors and develop them to make music a great art form and a profound medium of expression, and the way people use them to make and understand music.

MAKE IT ATTRACTIVE!

If general music class has been regarded in the past by many teachers as an unwelcome assignment, it is also evident that many pupils have approached it with less than active interest. Where a classroom is purposeful and attractive, pupils are likely to show an inclination to participate and learn more readily; where it is just another place to sit for an hour, it is likely that the pupils will approach it with exactly that attitude. Planning for the general music class requires the best a teacher has to offer in the way of knowledge of subject, materials, and pupils to be taught. A music room should look like a music room, not a social studies room, not a science room, not a room where any other subject is to be taught. The bulletin boards and the chalkboards should reflect this. The piano is only one instrument that can be placed advantageously in the room to make it attractive; Autoharps, demonstration instruments, and even discarded musical instruments can be used purposely for visual interest and instruction. But each item displayed should be more than displayed—it should be a functional part of the classroom, used in the live teaching of music.

MUSIC VS. THEORY: PRIORITY

The word "live" brings us to the heart of the general music problem. Whatever goes on in the music class should be functional first, theoretical second. Too often this has been reversed. Pupils with little or no interest in music have been forced to struggle with the copying of scales which they did not understand, key signatures which they could not use, and music terms for which they had no use. In some classes pupils have dissipated whatever interest they may have had in music through such activities as copying clef signs over and over again, drawing the staff, and learning abstract theory (e.g., a whole note equals four quarter notes).

In the mind of any pupil sitting in general music class one question should be paramount with regard to any piece of music information introduced by the teacher, and the same question should be uppermost in the mind of the teacher: "What difference does it make?" "What difference does it make that a treble clef is placed on five lines and four spaces?" "What difference does it make that the first line of the staff is E and the fifth line is F?" Is this fragmentary information which has no basis? Yes, probably, unless the student understands the whole apparatus, which is to say the Great Staff, and the diatonic scale. The Great Staff is a frame of reference for our system of the music notation; however, no one really needs to understand it unless he is going to make music with it. Making the music establishes the need for the staff, in the mind of today's pupil as in the mind of the inventor of the staff.

Here is another example of the theoretical versus the functional approach. Traditionally, instruments of the orchestra are taught by having the four families of the orchestra listed on the chalkboard while pupils copy and memorize them. Functionally, pupils should see and hear these instruments or at least know them, and the teaching should be pegged to such questions as, "*Why* do we have *four* stringed instruments, and what musical purpose is served by each of these?" Similar questions that develop the pupil's understanding of instruments of the orchestra might be, "What would happen to music if there were no trumpets?" and "Why do we need trombones?"

CURRICULUM CONTENT

A teacher who is committed to the teaching of general music classes must accept the total school population as having a legitimate place in such classes and must further accept the responsibility of developing significant musical experiences for students whose attitudes, interests, and abilities run the gamut. Sitting in these classes as a captive audience will be pupils with extremely limited musical background, while in the same classes there may be pupils who have had rich musical experiences including concert attendance and private music instruction. Certain pupils may never have seen musical notation—our American population is highly mobile and pupils transfer from schools with a negligible music program to schools with a highly developed music program. The teacher must be aware of the fact that, whatever the pupil's background and attitude, he is simply a reflection of what has, or has not, happened to him musically in the preceding years of his in-school and out-of-school experiences. In considering and accepting these differences, the teacher should begin to understand the significance and necessity of planning for everyone.

It is evident, then, that the general music course should be designed to service an *in*clusive rather than *ex*clusive pupil population, its content selected with a varied target population in mind—the relatively uninformed and unskilled, musically speaking, as well as those with more extensive musical backgrounds. Such a course should be predicated on a series of universally appealing musical experiences, with a hard core of musical knowledge and skill transmitted through such experiences, rather than on the basis of skill and knowledge supposedly acquired in *previous* music courses. The students participating in this course will bring to it a wide diversity of musical background, experience, and attitude, and the problem of reaching these students will have to be solved by creative, original, and inventive teachers who are able to break out of and go beyond traditional methods of presenting materials of appreciation. For example, the "today-we-study-sonata-form-and-learn-how-important-it-is" approach, which may be acceptable to a college class of the musically oriented would leave the class we are describing cold. Their attitude is more likely to be "Prove it!" than "Yes—do tell us."

In the junior high school years there are boys and girls eager to learn about music whose aesthetic "antenna" are extended in the hopes of receiving some arts signals that are intelligible, readable, and appealing. These pupils want us to help them like and understand music but because of previous unsuccessful experiences with music they appear antagonistic or, even worse, intimidated; the "I only know what I like" attitude is an example of the latter. These students will be represented in the junior high school music class.

Another group also will be represented—those who have developed a degree of skill in musical performance but who are woefully lacking in understanding of structure, literature, and style of music. This is a reiteration of what has been said often enough recently—a student may play the second clarinet part of a Bach fugue transcribed for band, do an adequate job, but know nothing either about Bach's specific contribution to music or about polyphonic music in general. An entire area of knowledge dealing with the composer's intent and the significance of his musical contribution awaits this group of students and may be revealed in the general music class. Both these students and the first group may be well serviced by the broadly based music course herein discussed.

The music class should include singing, playing, listening, and creating music, as well as demonstrations, field trips, use of filmstrips, films, television, assigned readings, and other relevant activities and experiences. All of these may serve to develop understanding of music through development of knowledge, skills, interests, and favorable attitudes.

The general music course should provide students with a background of musical knowledge and experience from which to develop perspectives with regard to the kinds of music heard in contemporary life (e.g., its origins, historical development), breadth of viewpoint on the many kinds of music available (e.g., the student who knows and likes only hillbilly music may be said to lack breadth of viewpoint, and this is also true of the student who knows and likes only opera), musical values with regard to choice of available musical materials and opportunities, and standards by which musical judgments may be formulated (e.g., "Did the choir perform well or only adequately? How do I know?").

The music class can help build skills, particularly in the aural comprehension of music, through a series of experiences selected and planned to lead from one to another. The study of individual instruments and choirs of the orchestra, for example, may lead to the study of the sound of the complete orchestra; the sound of singing voices and instruments are unmistakably different, but the differences lie within common property characteristics—timbre, loudness, duration, pitch; the study of the style of

Haydn may lead to that of Beethoven with regard to similarities and differences. And as the student learns to analyze, perceive, and discriminate among such experiences, he develops knowledge and understanding that equips him with the values and standards fundamental to a true appreciation of music.

A major purpose of education is to help the individual develop a sense of values with regard to the good, beautiful, and true in our society and way of life, to understand our heritage of great and enduring works, and to apply this knowledge to present performance and products. In any area of human affairs values develop through knowledge. If our youth are to develop musical values, they must learn the characteristics, media, and language of music and relate these to their musical experiences; the ability to discriminate and make quality judgments should follow.

PURPOSE, GOALS, AND IMPLEMENTING APPROACHES

Every activity in the general music class should have one overall purpose—the development of the musical intelligence of the pupil so that all the music he makes or hears will be more meaningful than it would have been without his participation in the class.

Under this general purpose we may list two paramount goals for all music teaching and learning:

1. For the learner to become more knowledgeable about, understanding of, and skillful regarding music. This includes listening, performing, discussing, and observing music, and any other interactions between it and the learner on a broad spectrum.
2. For the learner to enjoy music in an unself-conscious way. This may sound rather strange, certainly unusual, in the statement of a goal, but "unself-conscious" is exactly what is meant—the enjoyment of the musical art as part of one's everyday life, adding meaning, depth, self-fulfillment, and a dimension of the extraordinary, but accepted as a reasonable expectation for all individuals, rather than a special privilege of a minority.

Each one of us, in the achievement of these two goals, is somewhere on a continuum of zero to one hundred in the development of the processes leading to the goals. Probably a Toscanini or a Bernstein reaches a point close to one hundred (although it may be questioned whether the professional is ever "unself-conscious" about his art or discipline). Considering that we must accept the fact that pupils will enter the continuum at any point, being pushed into it from anywhere, or nowhere, from a musical, or non-musical, point of takeoff, it is a high expectation indeed that they should achieve status in the top portion of the distribution. This is particularly true when we realize that what musical foundation pupils have is often a factual, non-musical accumulation, rather than one resulting from planned immersion in music leading to musical learning and knowledge.

The above statements are meant to include all music in the pupil's environment, in-class and out-of-class music, in-school and out-of-school music. These are environmental experiences, generated by the total environment in which people find themselves from day to day. Certain of these are planned specifically for the pupil as an in-school experience and are therefore more or less controlled according to the teacher's musical intent, knowledge, experience, energy, and judgment. Others, however, are for the total population, and are commercially, rather than culturally, inspired. Such random experiences are readily available; they more or less saturate the environment. They are impelling and attract the pupil's attention because they are planned to do so.

Regardless of taste and culture, such musical actions surround the pupil through the forces of mass media, and although randomly experienced, they nevertheless leave their mark. They range from programs heard on "good music" FM radio stations to disc jockey programs playing the latest pop tunes. There is, of course, much more out-of-school music than in-school music consumed by pupils, simply because pupils are out of school many more hours a day than they are in school. To an increasing extent, it is believed that out-of-school musical experiences tend to shape musical taste, or at least to influence it. It therefore becomes obvious that every teacher of the general music class must cope with this phenomenon. The best teachers will recognize it, analyze it, and plan for constructive use of whatever segments seem appropriate.

How to plan constructive uses of such music is a problem for many teachers. The following suggestions may help:

1. Ask the class to discuss the various types of music that appeal to them. Avoid passing judgment; try to keep the discussion open and frank. As suggestions are forthcoming, list at the top of the chalkboard the music suggested by the class. *Include everything*, whether rock, pop, soul, country, or whatever.

2. Under each category ask students to describe the particular type of music listed. Keep the discussion moving in the direction of its *musical* characteristics.

3. Ask the class to help you make another list, this time with whatever criteria they think could be used for judging what makes any of this music good. Avoid placing a value judgment on the term "good." Again, it is important to keep this discussion open. Include in the list all items pupils give you as criteria for judging the "goodness" of music,

but feel free at this point to ask them to consider any additional criteria you wish to add. For example, is it important to think about how *long* a piece of music stays popular with its audience? Ask pupils whether they consider the pop tunes they liked a year or two ago to be good at this point. Ask them to consider approximately how long a popular song or piece of music remains popular.

4. Ask the class to list the best music they have heard in the past few months, using the criteria listed. At this point, it is useful to ask that they discuss what makes a good tune *good* and what causes the music to rate high in their opinion.

5. Ask pupils to consider what all of the music they have listed in (1) has in common. Try to get them to talk in terms of rhythmic characteristics (meter, tempo, accent), melodic and harmonic characteristics, types of instrument, notation, and, in the case of songs, solo characteristics and accompaniment.

Traditionally, the core of the general music class has been singing. This has placed an artificial boundary on the development of musical knowledge and limited the musical interests of all students, and for a reason that no longer is accepted—it was assumed that every student had a singing voice, could sing, and, furthermore, *wanted* to sing. Today the most successful general music classes feature a wide variety of musical experiences ranging from traditional singing to the formation of rock groups and the creation of electronic music. Every teacher should consider, list, and encourage as many musical activities as he believes he and his class can carry on together in the time available for the class to meet. It also seems evident that most teachers will have to learn more about certain musical activities pupils are interested in. Not many music teachers have a depth of knowledge concerning jazz, rock, country music, or soul, for example, but any interested teacher can acquire such knowledge by expending time and effort identifying and studying relevant materials.

2

Planning for Everyone

DEVELOPING THE MUSIC COURSE OF STUDY

For purposes of this discussion, first let's distinguish between "curriculum" and "course of study." The curriculum is the overall plan for the study of music in any particular school, whether elementary, middle, junior high, or senior high school. A course, as part of the curriculum, is a particular sequence of topics and materials organized as a course designed for a particular class or group. The overall curriculum embraces all courses of study in a particular school; the music curriculum embraces all music courses.

In projecting the curriculum for a given school, it is necessary to decide on a) all the courses that shall be offered, b) whether these courses shall be required or elective, c) what shall determine the qualifications of pupils for scheduling elective groups, and d) the time and credit allotment for each course. A broad rationale must be developed in terms of objectives for the curriculum. Such objectives should be considered in terms of characteristics of students entering the curriculum and the expected or hoped-for characteristics of students as they emerge from the curriculum. Basically, the required courses furnish the foundation of the curriculum, and some minimum expectations should be developed for all pupils on the basis of these courses; the superior outcome of the music curriculum in terms of musical expectancies should be the pupil who schedules not only basic but also elective courses. His exposure to music will be characterized by depth and persistence.

Since the music curriculum is the sum of all music courses, the heart of the curriculum has to lie in the way these courses are developed and taught. More time is spent developing courses of study often put on the shelf and unused than in most other school pursuits. Whether this is a profitable activity is debatable; however, the teachers engaging in it do need beginning guidelines. Some suggestions are as follows:

1. Decide on the objectives of the particular course being planned. List what children will be expected to learn, in terms of knowledge, understanding, musical skills. Certain objectives may be quite broad, of course, and may resemble the objectives for the total curriculum (e.g., to learn the sound of the orchestra). When we designate a particular skill to be acquired, however, we must become bore specific (e.g., to identify the instruments of the orchestra by sight and sound, or to distinguish the sound of the orchestra from that of the band). There certainly will be a relationship between general and specific objectives. The factual aspects of such matters may be considered cognitive, while the actual listening skill, although cognitive, also involves other domains. (A performing skill is likely to be in the psychomotor, cognitive, and affective domains.) In any case, all such expected results should be listed in terms of knowledge and skills. Thus the teacher knows what to expect of his pupils.[1]

2. The next step is to identify the body of musical content and the actual materials through which students will be expected to develop skills and knowledge. That is to say, one might learn rondo form through the music of Mozart, Schubert, or other composers. But in this case we must specify the particular musical compositions to be used in order to help the student develop a knowledge of form in music. Similarly, if we want the student to learn to read music, we must specify the objectives, methods, and materials. This portion of any course of study should be explicit and detailed but not inflexible.

3. The third step is to carefully work out the approximate number of periods available for the teaching of a particular course. For example, if a teacher has forty periods in which she can teach, she is more likely to be able to reinforce than if she has thirty periods; the student may hear a particular recording or sing a particular song more than once or twice. In making an analysis of the periods available, it is important to allow for teaching periods, review periods, and testing periods.

[1] Also see discussion of behavioral objectives, p. 25.

4. It is important to remember that the course of study should be organized in topics or units or otherwise arranged so that threads of continuity run through each topic, unit, or lesson and also through the entire course. Since music is to be studied, its basic elements and their musical extensions may be considered important threads of continuity.

ORGANIZING A MUSICAL UNIT OF STUDY

Whether you teach in terms of lessons, units, projects, musical problems, or other organized instructional segments, the unit is a familiar frame of reference; it should provide a major musical experience. In organizing the unit, try to follow some of these suggestions:

1. Decide whether or not the topic is important enough to be included as either a major or minor segment of the music course of study. Some topics are more appropriate as single lessons than as whole units.
2. Decide what musical elements will be better understood by the pupils through the musical experience planned, and how this is to be accomplished. What musical concepts do you expect students to develop?
3. a) Decide on the objectives, or the main focus, of the unit. For example, a unit on art songs might stress the relationship of the accompaniment (or accompanist) to the vocal line (or singer). This then would take precedence over discussion of the singer's style or voice type.
   b) Decide on the behavioral objectives of the unit. How do you and your pupils want their musical behavior to change as a result of their study?
4. List all materials needed to implement the unit objectives. Examine materials in detail to make sure the objectives will be well served and realized through the use of these particular materials.
5. Decide on the length of the unit, considering:
   a) Relative importance to entire course of study
   b) Materials available (songs, recordings, instruments)
   c) Class characteristics (background, intelligence, musical ability, and so forth)
   d) Length of class periods
   e) Teaching procedures (some procedures take more time than others); methods of presentation
6. Make a draft of the test to be given on the unit. This re-identifies the points to be stressed and should clarify objectives. Make sure the test relates to the objectives established.
7. Look at the entire topic from the pupil's viewpoint, rather than from the adult or skilled musician's viewpoint. Remember that he lacks your background—most of what you teach is new to him. Try to make sure he has the concepts needed to undertake a new project. For example,

a lesson on Ravel or another impressionist composer lacks meaning if your pupils have no concepts of impressionistic music.

8. Plan the lessons that will comprise the unit. Be sure to include a number of pupil-participation channels to generate musical activity.

9. It's important to remember that you cannot teach *everything* about any one topic, so decide on the major emphasis, the most important ideas and concepts. Check every lesson plan to be sure you are teaching what you planned to teach and what you will test.

MUSIC AS A DISCIPLINE: STRUCTURAL, CONCEPTUAL, BEHAVIORAL ASPECTS [1]

Key terms and phrases characterize every period of education, and music education is no exception. Examples of such terms are "structure," "basic elements," and "concepts." "Percepts" is also a popular term, and should be, since percepts furnish a sensory base for the development of concepts. Many of the articles and books that touch on the subject of musical concepts and elements reveal lack of agreement on terminology, or lack of precision in identifying elements. This handicaps music educators to such an extent that the newer members of the profession may have difficulty understanding and applying the ideas being conveyed.

The following pages discuss the nature of music as a subject discipline, the nature of concepts and concept formation (touched upon very briefly) and the ways in which children develop concepts of music, why it is desirable to teach from a conceptual basis of musical understanding and what pupils may gain thereby, the development of behavioral objectives, the activities vis-à-vis the concept-centered curriculum, and strategies for use of behavioral objectives.

MUSIC AS A DISCIPLINE

What is meant by music as a discipline? Briefly, that music is an area of knowledge, subject to its particular structure and governing regulations, which requires a special, differentiated approach to its teaching and learning where certain of its unique characteristics are concerned. That is to say, one who sets out to

[1] Portions of the material on pp. 17 to 25 are excerpted and adapted from a speech delivered by the author at Towson State College, Md., and included in a publication of that institution entitled *Disciplines Curriculum*, ed. Genevieve Heagney, 1964. Material is used by permission.

master music must follow different procedures from one who sets out to master painting.

For example, one cannot learn to play the piano in the same way one learns to paint. Each requires certain neuromuscular controls, but these differ, as do the media of performance. The continuum of music is silence; that of art, space. Think of a child experimenting with water colors—now think of a child experimenting with the piano keyboard. The differences are obvious. Another comparison: There are basic similarities in the processes of reading language and reading music. But there are great differences. (Eye movements are usually horizontal, but in some cases, as with piano, horizontal *and* vertical.) And the symbology of these two processes differs radically.

Music, one of the arts (an aural art as differentiated from a visual art), is implicitly interwoven with the human mind and spirit, concerning people both individually and collectively. Its texture, flavor, and aura are such that it must be produced and heard always with the understanding that heart, mind, body, soul, and spirit are involved, both of the maker and the receiver, the performer and the audience. Responses to music will always be on an emotional-intellectual basis, since its makers and listeners are human beings.

Consider a crude separation of these responses, by way of illustration: the emotional approach approximates, "I like it—I don't know or care why." Everyone does approach music sometime, somewhere, from this viewpoint. It is doubtful that even the most dedicated musician, for example, going down the aisle with his beloved bride to the strains of Mendelssohn would think to himself, "Ah-ha! Mendelssohn would have done better to use a dominant seventh right—*there!*"

The intellectual response is likely to approximate, "I appreciate this music because I understand it, because I am aware of what I like and do not like, and because I have a basis for justifying my opinion. It is possible for me to *like* certain music, however, even though I am cognizant that it is *not* 'good' music; it is also possible that I may dislike certain music even though I recognize its 'good' qualities."

ELEMENTS OF MUSIC

What is music? How can we describe it? How can we illuminate its meaning, clothe it with significance? Stranded on an alien planet, could we tell the curious natives what music is? Let's say we could not sing for them because they might interpret our sounds to represent either distress or threat; we could not pick up an instrument and sound it because they might think the instrument and accompanying gestures represented animosity. Now in such a situation, where ideas would need to be reduced to a point describing only the inherent structure of music, we would of necessity cite the inherent qualities and characteristics that constitute the basis of music as a discipline. In simplest terms, we might attempt to convey the idea through such a description as this:

Music moves higher and lower—that is, moving from higher pitches to lower pitches, vice versa, or remaining the same. Music has longer sounds and shorter sounds, changing from one to another, sometimes staying the same. Music has louder and softer sounds, changing from one to another, sometimes staying the same; it moves faster and slower, changes from faster to slower, and vice versa, and often moves at the same speed.

Notice that in addition to the characteristics listed, worded in terms pupils might understand, we must add analogies of timbre and, of course, form, thus heaping complexity upon complexity.

Certain characteristics of music have been described as having to do with the elements of pitch, duration, loudness, timbre. All of us know that these do not exist independently in a musical framework. They are the raw materials of music, and their subdivisions and various combinations make up the fine art of music. Fleming and Veinus describe them as follows:

To proceed now into the perception of qualities: pitch, perceived as the relative highness or lowness of two tones, is heard as a *line* moving upward or downward; duration, perceived as the relative longness or shortness of two tones, is felt as *meter;* intensity, perceived as the relative loudness or softness of two tones, is sensed as *dynamics;* while the distinction between timbres becomes the experience of *tone quality.* To go one step farther: the extension of linear movement becomes *melody;* the continuation of metrical movement becomes *rhythm;* the increase or decrease of intensities becomes *dynamics;* and the organization of timbres becomes *tone color.* Together the totality of this four-dimensional melodic, rhythmic, dynamic, and qualitative movement is the raw material of music, hence its fluidity and versatility as a medium of expression.[2]

In view of all this, it might be assumed that musicians and music educators would have no difficulty agreeing on the elements that underlie their discipline; such an assumption, however, appears not to be borne out in fact. An examination of the literature setting forth those elements of music to be learned, dealt with, or experienced by children not only reveals differences in terminology designations (e.g., tone color, timbre, texture), but also shows confusion in the designation of musical elements *per se*

2 William Fleming and Abraham Veinus, *Understanding Music* (New York: Holt, Rinehart and Winston, 1958), p. 7.

as differentiated from the musical extension of such elements. Sometimes a particular element is grouped with its extension or derivation (pitch and harmony); other times the element is omitted but the extension included (melody, harmony); rarely does a writer or speaker enumerate, classify, and define the elements that are basic and categorize their extensions clearly; for example, pitch, an element, has musical extensions in the form of melody and harmony.[3]

CONFUSION IN USAGE OF TERMS

If we try to fit the various definitions or listings of terms and elements into a basic format, the missing elements and/or the replications are evident. Yet elements are *fundamental in nature*. Therefore, if pitch is an element, harmony cannot also be an element, and neither can melody. Harmony and melody both derive from the pitch element of music and are musical extensions. It follows that melody and harmony should appear as sub-categories of pitch.

For example, where are loudness and timbre if a writer proposes as the elements of music rhythm, melody, harmony? Then too, we have the matter of form, sometimes mentioned as an element. Form is not really an element but is the organizational schemata of various musical elements as they combine into a communicative whole that is, of course, subject to great variance in terms of complexity and length. If music educators themselves show marked variations in identification, enumeration, and categorization and labeling of musical elements, it seems likely that pupils may show confusion in attaching correct labels to musical phenomena; some evidence exists that there is at least uncertainty.[4]

In view of the preceding discussion, it is evident that pupils should be given every opportunity to understand the musical elements listed in the chart on p. 27 through dealing with them in a musical context rather than by memorizing a definition of each.

Although musical elements in classroom discussion are often "translated"

[3] Frances M. Andrews and Ned C. Deihl, *Development of a Technique for Identifying Elementary School Children's Musical Concepts*. Cooperative Research Project No. 5-0233 (Washington: Office of Education, U.S. Department of Health, Education, and Welfare, 1967), p. 5.

[4] Andrews and Deihl, *Development of a Technique*, pp. 86, 87; Russell P. Getz, "The Influence of Familiarity through Repetition in Determining Optimum Response of Seventh Grade Children to Certain Types of Serious Music" (Unpublished doctoral dissertation, The Pennsylvania State University, 1963), p. 56; and Marilyn Pflederer Zimmerman and Lee Sechrest, *How Children Conceptually Organize Musical Sounds* (Cooperative Research Project No. 5-0256; Washington: Office of Education, U.S. Department of Health, Education, and Welfare, 1968), p. 137.

through such understandable comparisons and simile language as noted in the preceding discussion ("higher-lower" for pitch, "longer-shorter," "faster-slower" for duration, "louder-softer" for loudness), there is some evidence that children do not always grasp the idea of "higher" as applied to the pitch concept and "softer" as applied to loudness. And, as pointed out by Andrews and Deihl, there is much room for confusion in using these terms.[5]

In ordinary conversation parents instruct their children to "speak *up*" when they mean for them to speak louder, to "turn *down* the television set" when they mean that the volume should be decreased, to "*lower* your voice" when the intent is for the youngster to speak softer. A typical point of confusion was identified by Laverty [6] when she found that pupils could identify the softer musical passages and name them but could not label the louder passages with the same facility. (In considering this, it might be reasoned that children learn "soft" and "hard" as opposites, but that in musical application "soft" applies, but not "hard" as. the opposite.) Children need to be taught the correct terminology in the context of its musical application.

However, music first becomes part of us, part of children, as a vital total experience, not as a structured discipline. Therefore, in the process of developing children's key understandings, we must be careful not to strip music of its primary appeal as a whole, integrated, joyously presented art form. We must first acquaint the child with the impact of music. Then by expanding this understanding of music's nature, our task must be to direct him along the path of developing a critical, questioning sense of musical values based on enjoying and understanding music.

It is the phase of *understanding* music that has been unintentionally neglected in the schools. For enjoyment does not necessarily lead to understanding and appreciation; sometimes it leads to passive, undiscriminating, uncritical acceptance. The beginnings of appreciation may deteriorate into *depreciation;* it is perhaps possible that music has become so much of the apperceptive background of life today that it is not appreciated. There is reason to believe that mass media have been developing *depreciation* rather than *appreciation* of music.

The school must, by the very fact that it has highly limited time with children but seemingly a vast, unlimited accumulation and range of what to teach (with more being added each year through the knowledge explosion), carefully select and choose its curriculum content. It must assign priority values to certain selected areas of this content; otherwise, teach-

---

5 Andrews and Deihl, *Development of a Technique,* pp. 86, 87.
6 Grace E. Laverty, "The Development of Children's Concepts of Pitch, Loudness, and Duration as a Function of Grade Level" (Unpublished doctoral dissertation, The Pennsylvania State University, 1969), p. 70.

ers and learners both are likely to undergo a mutually frustrating educational experience.

The stress or thrust, it would seem, must therefore be in the direction of emphasis on developing concepts of the elements or raw materials that make up music as a discipline, and how they function.

How do children develop concepts? According to David Russell,

> . . . concepts develop out of related perceptual experiences and as a result of the child's reorganization of experiences in a problem-solving or creative way. . . . Not only generalization but discrimination is involved. . . . Many perceptual experiences may precede the verbalization. Accordingly, the new concepts . . . usually involve verbal responses which represent a certain amount of generalization and discrimination. They are less commonly non-verbal. In some experiments, children show clear understanding of a concept but inability to verbalize it. In any case, the concept represents a class or group, or one aspect of a class or group, usually with a label attached to it, rather than an individual instance.
>
> . . . .
>
> One agreement among all psychologists concerns the importance of concepts in the child's and the adult's thinking. The clarity and completeness of a child's concepts are the best measure of his probable success in school learning because meaning is fundamental to such learning. The adult's concepts determine pretty well what he knows, what he believes, and thus in large part what he does.[7]

Relating to the thrust in the direction of developing musical concepts, consider one within easy grasp of pupils' understanding. While it is difficult to divorce a child's understanding of tempo in music from loudness or intensity, the matter of loudness may be discussed rather simply within the musical context of a lullaby. At one time or another many children are sung to by parents eager to comfort them or to quiet them into sleep. Through this experience children absorb the idea that one sings a lullaby in a certain fashion—they develop this idea through listening to someone singing this type of song. (It may very well be, too, that they role-play the idea with dolls and other toys.) In first group-singing attempts, however, children do not differentiate particularly with regard to singing at a relatively loud or soft level. They sing, and this is as it should be. We then help them develop awareness of the fact that a range of loudness or dynamics is employed in music by directing attention to this in connection with singing a lullaby. When they have learned a lullaby, they are asked to consider whether it should be sung softly or loudly, in terms of the sound their voices produce, and perhaps give a few examples. There is never much question about the response—they think it surprising that a

[7] Reprinted by permission of the publisher, from David H. Russell, *Children's Thinking* (Waltham, Massachusetts: Blaisdell Publishing Company, A Division of Ginn and Company, 1956), pp. 117, 118, 120.

lullaby might be sung loudly. Lullabies are sung softly because they have a particular function in the scheme of things. Thus we draw from the child's experience his own readiness to understand a basic musical concept. But we cannot stop here; we must then proceed to compare this with a musical experience in which a louder sound is desirable.

It is certain that each of us forms concepts; it is also clear that these are sometimes erroneous or confused. The pupil who stated that the hornpipe was something sailors smoked when bored was confusing dancing with the use of tobacco. The youngster who thought Debussy was an "oppressionistic" composer may have been confusing music with tyranny. These answers point up an unfortunate emphasis in music teaching as well as in the teaching of other subjects: a share, at least, of school-directed learning about music consists of verbal memorizations and mechanical performances that do *not* enlighten the learner as to the real nature of music. At times we appear to be frozen into a static pattern of teaching music, full of procedures that possess the potential for effectively *preventing* the learner from developing musical concepts.

One of the more persistent complaints of music educators is that children do not learn to read music with any significant degree of skill. Yet upon reflection it would appear that we put definite obstacles in the path of developing such skill by failure to help the learner structure a basis for understanding this involved process and its function.

The diatonic scale is the frame of reference for music in western civilization and is a starting point as music is presented in the schools. This scale is therefore the basis for beginning music reading. It is a *system* made up of a discrete *series* of musical sounds—pitches. We can actually consider the scale *concept* outside the context of musical dimensions, simply as an idea in itself. We have every opportunity to develop the child's understanding of the scale both as an abstraction and as a musical experience.

This is a seven-note scale, the eighth note repeated as an octave unison of the first. Therefore the series may be designated by seven numbers in sequence, seven letters of the alphabet in sequence, or seven arbitrarily chosen symbols derived from any other systematic order. Once having acquainted youngsters with the *sound* of the sequence-system in a musical context—that is, learned in association with its designated symbol *and* pitch—it is not difficult to explain that the seven numbers, letters, or whatever, are used because a relationship does exist among these sounds and their symbols and that they do form an overall grouping known as a scale. There is a psychological basis for teaching this way, since expectation is part of the learning set—that is, if we sing several notes in sequence, the learner expects a certain note, or notes, to follow in the scheme. He is already half-persuaded that the scheme exists and has real being. The completion of his expectation is the conclusion of his part-knowledge. Perhaps it is in this critical stage—"closure"—that we are most lackadaisical in our teaching.

The obstacles placed in the path of the learners, considering once more the whole process of music reading as an example, are also well illustrated by the "straitjacket" presentation of the music staff. Youngsters are often introduced to this framework of music notation somewhat casually in the first grade, where they are shown songbooks, sometimes in color and illustrated, which may not always serve to attract attention to the music staff and symbols. Other youngsters are formally introduced to the music staff and are taught that "every good boy does fine," and "face," may be associated with five lines and four spaces. This may not do much to encourage real understanding of either music or conduct.

It is also interesting to note that, however the music staff is introduced in the elementary school, children are not often told the whole story; the treble clef staff alone is usually presented in the elementary school, and of course it is only part of the story. Usually the child does not learn about the bass clef staff until he is in junior high school (piano and certain other instrumental students excluded). Yet it is rather clear to see, analyzing the situation, that having the picture of the Great Staff in front of the learner clarifies the whole situation. He can see the progression of letter names, line, space, line, space, line space, line space, line, through middle C and beyond.

Failure to explain middle C is an example. We skip over too many such connecting links, links that are needed to throw light on the structure of music; we teach too many dry, unrelated facts that, lacking significance, are readily forgotten.

In conclusion, let us take a look at the end results. What is to be gained from teaching music as a discipline? What will pupils gain from a conceptual approach to musical learning?

1. First, music becomes understandable to all. When an individual says, "I don't know anything about music; I only know what I like," he reveals that he has been denied a gift of knowledge, one that should have enriched his education and his in-school and out-of-school life. The approach advocated would minimize this situation.

2. Second, there are certain standards of musical expectation that may be applied by any performer, creator, or listener. These constitute normative, qualitative standards. For example, although the tone quality of violinists differs, displaying individual characteristics, no one may do *violence* to the essential violin tone and avoid stepping over certain lines of good taste. These norms or standards may be taught to and understood by all to some degree.

3. Music is a flexible, fluid medium of expression with great room for individual differences in performance. This flexibility must be under-

stood by the intelligent performer and the intelligent listener, since it constitutes the essence of the art of music. Understanding the *use* and *misuse* of this flexibility develops from a sound understanding of the art of music.

4. Music has a comparatively long and priceless art heritage to communicate to each generation; we have a sound musical basis for approaching this through its inherent structure.

Finally, approaching music as a discipline implies that we will communicate the fact that the study of music involves more than passive reception, more than a simple emotional response. It implies that music does have substance which, if understood, affects all men's capacity to receive and to communicate this priceless medium of human expression.

DEVELOPMENT OF BEHAVIORAL OBJECTIVES

As we become more specific in expecting certain measurable changes to occur as the result of learning, we begin to identify and set up objectives representing musical behavior believed to be applicable to and useful in the out-of-school present and future life of pupils. The formulation of such behavioral objectives must follow the recognition of ways in which music functions in present-day society, has functioned in past societies, and is effective in our lives. It is unrealistic to reject many of the roles pupils see music playing in their everyday existence, to accept and approve only a few traditional ones. We may not like all the music our pupils like, but this is not sufficient grounds for showing a negative attitude toward it as opposed to their positive attitude. No classroom should constitute a battlefield on which teachers and pupils have head-on collisions over what is or is not good music. The battle to develop musical values is not won this way. Whether or not we like it, the music surrounding pupils, heard via mass media, is furnishing musical models which many find acceptable and even engrossing, as witness the amount of money spent each year on records other than those featuring baroque, classical, romantic, impressionistic, expressionistic, modern, contemporary, and electronic music. It is realistic to help pupils identify other, different, musical models that are less obvious in their appeal and work toward an understanding of ways in which such music has a place in today's world—not only because it has endured, but because it still possesses relevance and intrinsic value.

It is obvious that music education must be broad enough to meet the needs of three groups: the professionals of the future, the musical amateurs, and those who will be chiefly consumers—that is to say, the audience.

These groups have different needs and goals, therefore different objectives. Some objectives, though, will apply to all three groups, some to two groups, and still others to only one group. For example, it seems likely that everyone would find it musically useful to recognize the sound of the orchestra as differentiated from that of the band. It seems likely that both musical professional and amateur need to know how to sight read music, with the professional needing a much more highly-developed skill than the amateur. But many future audience members will probably get along fairly well without any great emphasis on their music reading competence, just as many people drive automobiles competently every day without understanding exactly what goes on under the hood.

The development of behavioral objectives should be related to concept-centered learning, and a cyclical sequence of teaching and learning experiences.* These, of course, must be rooted in musical experiences.

All of the preceding may be summarized by saying that pupils have a real and pressing need to believe in the reality of the school as a force that is part of, rather than *apart from*, their lives. They need daily demonstrations testifying that the substance of their in-school experience has an in-life application. The work of Asahel Woodruff is eloquent testimony to this, and that of Mager is also supportive. Both make it clear that objectives must be formulated in terms that can be clearly stated, understood, and implemented in terms of pupil competence.[8] Woodruff is insistent that the pupil's will to accomplish is a strong motivation, and believes that this motivation is a predeterminer of the pupil's acceptance of a particular objective and his success in achieving it.[9] He holds that pupils learn constantly from the in-life, out-of-school world, but that learning is interrupted by the in-school situation—the nine-to-three part of the day—because of unreal, non-behavioral objectives. This too often frustrates the pupil and is a cause of negative attitudes toward school.[10]

The following chart illustrates the substance of music in relation to its makers and users. To be involved with music as a meaningful whole,

---

* A discussion of "cyclical sequence" may be found in an article by James L. Mursell entitled "Growth Processes in Music Education," *Basic Concepts in Music Education*, The Fifty-Seventh Yearbook of the National Society for the Study of Education, Part I, ed. by Nelson B. Henry (Chicago: University of Chicago Press, 1958), pp. 157-60.

[8] Asahel D. Woodruff, *First Steps in Developing a New School Program*, rev. ed. (Salt Lake City: Bureau of Educational Research, University of Utah, 1968), p. 15; Robert F. Mager, *Preparing Instructional Objectives* (Palo Alto: Fearon Publishers, Inc., 1962), p. 1.

[9] Asahel D. Woodruff, "Preconference Educational Research Training Project in Music Education, 1969: Blue Papers," pp. 2, 3. Mimeographed.

[10] Woodruff, *First Steps*, pp. 5, 6; Asahel D. Woodruff and Janyce L. Taylor, *A Teaching Behavior Code*, M-Step Monograph No. 3 (Salt Lake City: Utah State Board of Education, 1968), p. 12.

the pupil must deal with each of the aspects identified, whether in the role of audience member or performer. It shows the elements of music, certain of their musical extensions and characteristics, the media of music, and the roles of people who are involved with music. The interrelationships of these variables are infinite, but until our pupils grasp at least the meaning and significance of the items shown and how they interrelate, no objective basis for understanding the structure of music or its meaningful relationship to society has been established. This in turn means that pupils will have no foundation for formulating musical values, taste, and judgments.

A CHART OF SOME MUSICAL ELEMENTS, EXTENSIONS, CHARACTERISTICS, AND AREAS
TO BE EMPHASIZED IN A GENERAL MUSIC CLASS

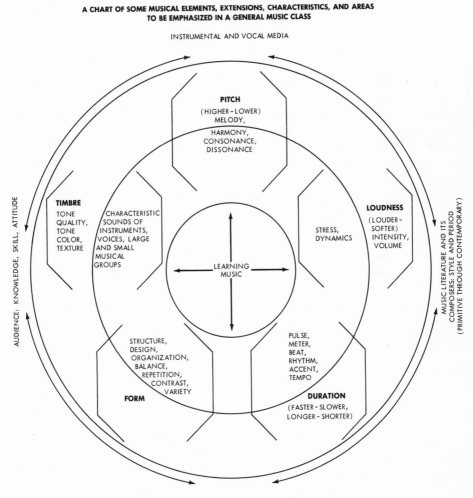

INSTRUMENTAL AND VOCAL MEDIA

PITCH
(HIGHER - LOWER)
MELODY,
HARMONY,
CONSONANCE,
DISSONANCE

TIMBRE
TONE
QUALITY,
TONE
COLOR,
TEXTURE

CHARACTERISTIC
SOUNDS OF
INSTRUMENTS,
VOICES, LARGE
AND SMALL
MUSICAL
GROUPS

LEARNING
MUSIC

LOUDNESS
(LOUDER -
SOFTER)
INTENSITY,
VOLUME

STRESS,
DYNAMICS

STRUCTURE,
DESIGN,
ORGANIZATION,
BALANCE,
REPETITION,
CONTRAST,
VARIETY

FORM

PULSE,
METER,
BEAT,
RHYTHM,
ACCENT,
TEMPO

DURATION
(FASTER - SLOWER,
LONGER - SHORTER)

AUDIENCE: KNOWLEDGE, SKILL, ATTITUDE

MUSIC LITERATURE AND ITS
COMPOSERS: STYLE AND PERIOD
(PRIMITIVE THROUGH CONTEMPORARY)

PERFORMERS: STYLE, TECHNIQUE, INTERPRETATION, MUSICIANSHIP

EXPLANATION OF CHART
OF MUSICAL ELEMENTS

The rationale for the chart is intended to be interpreted as moving from the basic learner position through the characteristics of musical elements and their various extensions, manifestations, combinations, and transformations to the people involved in composing, performing, and consuming music, a circle that also includes the various vocal and instrumental media. However, the chart could be adapted to move from the *people* and *media* shown in the outer circle through the basic elements, if the importance of the learner and the learning of music are borne in mind. The learner himself and the various musical phenomena are important variables.

It is possible that the items noted on the chart could be used in any sequence or combination the teacher believes effective in the classroom or in any other musical situation. It could be greatly extended in detail by the individuals using it, and possibly reorganized in various forms as an interesting exercise by teacher or class in understanding how all possible combinations and variations of musical phenomena evidence themselves. The teacher should deal with each of the areas recognized in the chart in some effective, musical way so pupils will understand the structure of music and, at least in part, its logic as a discipline as well as its greatness as an art form.

EXAMPLES OF
BEHAVIORAL OBJECTIVES

1. The student will describe the difference between any two of the tempo indications Lento, Andante, and Allegro, and illustrate in 4/4 meter by playing, singing, moving, or tapping.
2. The pupil will listen as the teacher plays a familiar song in four different tempi, and will use the correct tempo term in identifying each rendition. He will then choose the one most appropriate tempo for the song.
3. From a list of six given folksongs familiar to the student, he will a) correctly identify each as a worksong, fo'csle chantey, or spiritual, and b) sing or play any two with appropriate expression (tempo and dynamics).
4. Given a tape recording of twenty orchestral instruments, the student will be able to identify fifteen by name and orchestral family after no more than two hearings.
5. The student will listen to six compositions by different composers and correctly identify each after one hearing.

6. Given a list of musical characteristics describing the styles of composers of musical compositions played by the orchestra during the school year, the orchestra members will list the composer and title of composition corresponding to each.
7. The student will select music appropriate to a class play set in the period of the Civil War.
8. The student will recognize aurally (without score) and identify the following: music written in 4/4, 3/4, and 6/8 meter.
9. The student will examine the music of an unfamiliar song and mark in the appropriate tempo (or tempi if this changes in the course of the song), dynamics, and other indications of expressive rendition.
10. Using the letters A, B, C, etc., the student will listen to a composition in rondo form and write the letters designating themes in proper order as they occur or recur.

The study of musical elements and media as shown on the chart involves various aspects—emotional and/or aesthetic (affective domain), intellectual (cognitive domain), manipulative or skill-centered (psychomotor domain). All of these bear upon the evolution of musical tastes and values; any or all may help the individual develop a sense of appreciation, to use a now out-of-favor term but one which conveys general meaning. We need to ask ourselves constantly, then, and encourage our pupils to focus attention on, how and why music makes us feel and respond as it does; what, how, and why music makes us think; and in sum, how music makes us feel, think, and respond. How and why does a particular musical composition affect us a certain way? Are we aware of and receiving the musical intent of the composer as we listen to and/or perform his music? Such questions lead to examination and consideration of the basic musical characteristics of a work, as opposed to attention to superficial facts about it.

Consider, for example, that a composer begins with an idea. He creates, because of the idea, a musical problem to be solved as he places this idea in the language of music. As he composes, he solves problems of form, melody, harmony, meter, rhythm, and a host of additional musical matters relevant to the composition that is emerging. He also creates problems for the performer, who must solve them through recreating the music. These involve technical facility, interpretation, knowledge of the composer's style, and the ability to make a musical, communicative performance. Even the listener, the consumer, is involved in the entire problem-solving process, because he receives and interprets the message of the composer (as the performer conveys it) in his own mode of response, on his own "wave length." His reception is limited in terms of his "receiving set," which comprises a package—knowledge, skill, attitude, interest, receptivity. This package is the receiving set, mentally and emotionally.

If we can help our pupils find the answers to the musical problems faced and solved by both composer and performer, they will have an improved chance of developing the musical values so important in terms of what is called good taste and judgment. In other words, it is more likely that we will develop the educated, erudite, and knowledgeable audience which has been lacking in the United States.

ACTIVITIES CURRICULUM, CONCEPT-CENTERED CURRICULUM, BEHAVIORAL OBJECTIVES

What about the so-called activities curriculum vis-à-vis the concept-centered curriculum? There is no difficulty in reconciling the two; the concept-centered curriculum is a way of attaining the big ideas, the great basics that are the underlying structure of understanding music as an art and a subject discipline; the activities approach should implement and help develop the concepts. For example, learning to strum an accompaniment on the guitar may lead to the concept of tone quality (timbre) of the guitar, loudness appropriate to an accompaniment, harmonic aspects of pitch as used to accompany a melody, tone quality contrasts of voice and guitar, rhythmic concepts, and on and on—IF the teacher will reveal these. The problem with the activities curriculum is that it too often stops with the activities, while the concepts curriculum may fail to extend into the activities that both implement it and hold the interest and attention of the young pupil.

It should be evident, therefore, that the two complement each other well, particularly when organized from a behavioral objectives basis. That is, the musical activities in which young people are usually engaged, or indicate a desire to be engaged, are the building blocks of both concept-centered and activities curricula. Organized in terms of behavioral objectives, the particular activity provides motivation and drive, the necessary power source for the pupils. A competent teacher, having discovered the motivating activities, will determine the appropriate behavioral objectives, identify relevant concepts, and map the achievement route for the pupil; the task then becomes to some degree self-directed. A more traditional approach, less pupil-centered, may take either concepts or objectives as a point of departure. This approach is more contrived, however, and fails to utilize pupil power in its most attractive and engaging state. The three strategies that follow are variations on the work of Asahel Wooddruff, who, however, is committed to an in-life approach.[11]

[11] Woodruff, *First Steps,* pp. 38, 39.

Three Strategies for Working with Behavioral Objectives and Concept-Directed Learning

Strategy I
(a) Identify musical activities that are of interest to pupils.
(b) Derive and describe in operational terms behavioral objectives that may be achieved through activities identified.
(c) Determine concepts needed for achievement of objectives.
(d) Predict major learnings that will evolve from preceding.
(e) Implement the preceding.
(f) Evaluate.

Strategy II
(a) Establish and describe in operational terms behavioral objectives (normative).
(b) Determine concepts necessary for achievement of objectives.
(c) Predict major learnings that will evolve from preceding.
(d) Identify musical activities that will accommodate process of developing the preceding; implement.
(e) Evaluate.

Strategy III
(a) Identify concepts needed by pupils to develop musical knowledge and values.
(b) Derive and describe in operational terms behavioral objectives that will accommodate concomitant development of concepts.
(c) Identify musical activities that will lead to achievement of (a) and (b).
(d) Predict major learnings that will evolve from preceding.
(e) Implement.
(f) Evaluate.

EVALUATION: THE MEASUREMENT OF ACHIEVEMENT

"If it can be taught, it can be tested. If it can be learned, it can be tested." For years the arts have labored under the illusion that their content, by and large, *cannot* be tested. This may be true in part, but neither can the total impact of any subject on the learner. What has happened in music with regard to measuring achievement? Probably two things. The first is that those teachers who have believed their teaching could not be measured have tended to teach in musical generalities, hoping that their pupils were developing "appreciation." Second, others have tried to test, but in a misdirected effort have tested the least important items—names and works of composers, lists of instruments, identification of lines and spaces, names of operatic characters, and other bits and pieces of non-musical information. Over the years children have filled countless notebooks with such non-musical bits and pieces. Very seldom has information of this kind and tests based upon it revealed much about the musical knowledge, understanding, or skill possessed by a child. Here are some typical examples of non-musical questions.

1. "Name the four instruments of the string section of the orchestra." (He may be able to name them and still know nothing of their sound and musical function.) A musical question on this topic might be: "You have heard the musical sound produced by the four stringed instruments. Listen to a melody I will play on the piano, and tell which instrument would play it best in terms of its pitch." (Teacher plays soprano melody.) "If you want this melody to be played by the next lowest stringed instrument, which instrument would that be?"

2. "How many counts are there in a measure of 4/4 meter?" This question is an exercise in arithmetic.) A musical question on this topic might be: "You are going to hear eight measures of music played in 4/4 meter. How many counts do you hear in each measure?"

or

"I will play three songs we have sung in class. Indicate whether No. 1, No. 2, or No. 3 is in 4/4 meter."

3. "Match the names of the composers given in Column I with the compositions listed in Column II." (This is purely factual information.) A "musical memory" contest type of question would ask for the matching *and* the recognition. But a better type of question might give a list of composers and then ask students to listen to and match unfamiliar compositions with the composer's name. This implies that the student has learned to recognize the composer's style.

4. "Define *fortissimo, lento* (and other musical terms as given)." A musical version might be: "You will hear a passage played in which there is a change from 'piano' to a softer *or* louder level of dynamics. From the list of terms given, choose the one that is appropriate to the change you hear."

5. "Which of the following instruments is played with a bow: trumpet, 'cello, clarinet, ukulele?" A musical version might be: "Draw a line through the errors in the following paragraph: The trumpeter rosined his bow carefully before playing *Taps* so that he would not fluff the highest note. As he did this, he could hear a clarinetist strumming 'Dixie' on his clarinet, using a reed as a strummer."

or

"Describe the difference in tone caused by bowing a violin as compared to plucking its strings."

6. "List three keyboards that preceded the pianoforte and one composition written for each." A question that would reveal the impact of the invention of the pianoforte on music might be: "How did the invention of the pianoforte affect the style of compositions written for keyboard?" Another type of question might be: "A composer wishes to write a composition that will call for sustained chords and a marked variation in dynamics from very loud to very soft. Will he choose to compose this for virginal, clavichord, harpsichord, or pianoforte, and why?"

The general principle involved in the preceding examples is one that is honored more often in the breach than in the observance, but nevertheless holds true—every question on music should be about and derived from a musical experience. Knowing the characters in an opera and the roles played is important to us only as the composer portrayed them musically; how the music reveals them in a particular way is his contribution to music. If a youngster, after studying *Carmen,* can explain why the composer wrote the fiery "Habanera" for Carmen and not for Micaela, he has developed some musical insights. Thus, the teacher's problem is to be perceptive in forming such questions so they will *reveal* and *reinforce* musical learning. In other words, the best questions are based on, but *lead beyond,* the musical experiences of pupils and should help the pupil develop musical concepts instead of isolated bits and pieces.

Why is evaluation an important part of the teaching-learning process? Chiefly because it is imperative that the pupil recognize his progress, realize what he has learned, be informed as to his achievement. What has been learned from programed instruction alone indicates the value of such feedback as a source of information and motivation. But superior teachers have known for many years that recognition of accomplishment, whether in the form of a smile, a word of praise, or a good test grade, possesses magic. Notice that the examples are positive; teachers are often prone to recognize only errors, too pressed for time to stop and comment, "That was a good answer," or "How did you come up with that idea so fast?" (Music educators are likely to believe this if they recall how often they were told about *errors* during a lesson, or allowed to play or sing with no comment, and how rarely stopped because a passage had been well performed.) *Achievement deserves recognition.*

Programed instruction has taught us something else—that great skill and perception are required to formulate good questions and that the idea is to produce questions pupils *can* answer correctly. This assumes that if material has been well developed and presented, the pupil should be able to furnish correct answers. Responsibility is thus placed on the teacher's ability to elicit a high percentage of correct answers in response to his question, for otherwise the pupil's intelligence and industry are not the only factors suspect—the teacher's ability to communicate knowledge is under question.

WHAT QUESTIONS DO YOU ASK?

A fairly good index for evaluating teaching might be the kind of questions a teacher asks, rather than the answers given. We can accept the fact that every worthwhile musical question should derive from a musical experience, but implementing this as part of our teaching philosophy is another matter entirely.

Asking when Bach was born and died is easy; no thought goes into asking or answering that question. But many were born and died in this same period. The questions that matter are, for example: "What difference would it have made if Bach had been born in 1485 rather than 1685? What did he accomplish in the years between his birth and death that made him different from other musicians living in the same approximate time period? Listen to the following composition by Bach and tell whether you think it is played by the musical instrument(s) for which he wrote it, or transcribed for other instruments. You will hear five compositions by various composers. Indicate which are in the style Bach used most." (Teacher plays five compositions, three in polyphonic, two in homophonic style.)

Examples of additional questions that encourage the pupil to recall his musical experiences follow:

1. The church music committee is deciding whether to buy a piano or a small organ to be played during church services. Which would be better for congregational singing? For playing a prelude and postlude to the service? Why?

2. In the unit on marches, we heard two wedding marches, one by Wagner and one by Mendelssohn. The Wagner march is traditionally used as a processional and the Mendelssohn as a recessional at weddings. Describe the musical characteristics that make this appropriate for the two marches. Could you reverse the roles of the two marches?

3. How is the sound of a band different from that of an orchestra?

4. Of all the musical instruments you have heard, which do *you* consider the best for wakening a heavy sleeper? Give three reasons that relate to the sound of the instrument.

5. Could you write a singable national anthem in polyphonic style? If so, how; if not, why not?

6. We heard examples of a violin being played *pizzicato* (plucking strings) and *arco* (bowing strings). Listen to five examples of *pizzicato* and *arco* playing and indicate which style of playing is being used:

   1. _____ 2. _____ 3. _____

   4. _____ 5. _____

WAYS OF GAINING ACTIVE PUPIL PARTICIPATION

Many pupils evidence lack of interest in music because they do not feel involved with it. Those who are in instrumental or choral organizations or are learning to play an instrument perceive their musical roles quite clearly, but the self-image of others seems to be less readily identified. While activity and involvement are not synonymous, one sometimes leads to the other, and ways of developing active roles for the pupils in music class are limited only by the teacher's imagination.

The following is a list of ways through which even disinterested pupils may be encouraged to participate:

1. Use a variety of rhythmic activities without rhythm instruments. Pupils may be asked to snap fingers, brush one hand against the other, click tongue, use cupped hands, or make other incisive sounds that will aid in establishing rhythm. Also try using a combination of hand sounds and such sounds as slapping knees, sliding feet, toe-heel or heel-toe tapping, stamping, stamp-clapping, stamp-sliding, and other combinations. These are useful in helping children feel the swing of a song or determine the meter of a song. Objective: developing sensitivity to pulse, beat, meter.

2. Through the use of rhythm instruments, active participation may be gained. A large variety of rhythm instruments is available and includes such simple devices as sticks, claves, gourds, and tone blocks. More formal instruments such as snare or bass drum may also be used. Here the pupil should concentrate on choosing appropriate instruments, deciding where to use such instruments to achieve the best musical effect (try having pupils play all instruments "tutti" for sixteen measures or so, and they will soon see that this is a deadening *and* deafening activity), and where to distribute the playing of instruments over a song so that it will best add to the metrical effect through determining where the accents and phrases fall. Objective: developing sensitivity to use of rhythm instruments singly or in combination.

3. A good way to develop rhythmic activity is by using the Autoharp to stress the rhythmic patterns of song accompaniments, deciding where an entire chord will be played using all the strings and where only the lower or upper strings will be played, determining how to combine or alternate such styles of playing and how many times a chord should be played in a measure or phrase; locating accents; and experimenting with the various possible tone qualities appropriate to different songs or rhythmic activities in terms of volume and style of playing. Objective: exploring musical potential of the Autoharp as an accompanying instrument.

4. Resonator bells may be used to good advantage in order to explain the scale concept, construct chords, and make chording accompaniments to songs. Bottles filled with different amounts of water are excellent "instruments" for explaining basic pitch concepts since the pupil can easily see what is taking place. Objective: stated in first sentence.

5. a) Orchestral instruments that can be simply played are useful in the classroom, such as string bass or 'cello used for plucking a simple harmonic or rhythmic accompaniment. Actually, even the violin or

viola might be bowed or plucked as a type of drone "bass" (in this case, drone alto or soprano) accompaniment. Some teachers like to detune the 'cello or bass and play it as a rhythmic accompaniment. Objective: using real orchestral instruments in ways that are within the capability of musical neophytes.

b) Use of such so-called social instruments as ukulele, banjo, guitar should not be overlooked. They are attractive as accompanying instruments for group singing, and have potential for arousing interest and participation. Almost any student can quickly learn to accompany a two-chord song on these instruments. Objective: constructive use of these instruments in classroom.

6. Piano and chord organ are excellent for developing chording ability, ostinato parts, and some of the activities in (4) or (5). Objective: constructive use of these instruments in classroom.

7. The tape recorder, a fascinating instrument for most junior high school pupils, may be constructively used to record any of the above activities. Ask pupils to listen critically to their own performance; it is important that the teacher and pupils identify the good characteristics of the performance as well as the ways in which it may be improved. Objective: developing a critical sense of musical performance.

8. An activity which is of interest to some pupils is the use of conducting patterns to locate the accent in a song and determine the meter signature. This should not be taught as abstract information but should be definitely associated with learning a piece of music. Objective: associating conductor's beat with musical function.

9. When the teacher plays an introduction to a song, pupils are often interested in counting or conducting the measures of the introduction and determining when they should begin singing, without a signal from the teacher. Objective: following a musical score as written for piano.

10. Using a metronome to develop concepts of tempo is a good way to engage a class in the activity of adjusting the instrument to various speeds. Be sure to develop this in connection with judging the tempo at which a particular song should be sung. Have pupils work with setting the metronome at a tempo indication appropriate to songs being sung. Objective: developing awareness of tempo markings in relation to musical function.

11. a) During listening lessons, focus attention on identification of various themes in the composition by placing them on the chalkboard in *scrambled* order and asking pupils to unscramble and identify in *correct* order. Objective: developing music reading activity.

b) A similar procedure may be followed with lists of instruments to be heard in a musical composition. Objective: drawing attention of pupils to instrumental characteristics of a composition.

12. The use of listening guides, prepared by the teacher, elicits pupil reaction during the listening itself. (Be sure these are guides, not tests. The *test* is a recall of information, or an application of knowledge already learned. The guide is a means of acquiring the informa-

tion or knowledge.) Objective: focusing attention and highlighting musical characteristics of the composition heard.

13. Pupils may identify, notate, and play characteristic rhythm patterns on appropriate instruments after hearing a musical composition. Objective: developing listening acuity; using and translating notation into musical action.

14. From a choice of several meter signatures, a pupil may identify the correct meter signature and indicate such identification by clapping or conducting it for the *class* to identify. This may also be used by the teacher playing a series of songs known by the class and asking for meter identification. Objective: developing awareness of meter.

15. Experiment with regular orchestral instruments—let pupils try to produce tones, discover ways of varying pitches and loudness. Objective: discovering ways in which musical sounds are produced and varied.

16. Electronic music is a field in which many junior high school students have involved themselves with almost compulsive interest and a high degree of self-motivation. Objective: comparing two modes of sound production—musical instruments and electronically-produced sounds.

17. Aleatory music: Involve the class, or groups within the class, in creating a musical composition of sounds that are produced from musical instruments and/or other sounds (sounds made by use of hands, feet, pencils, rulers, books, or other environmental sources). Pupils should combine these sounds in a chance or random arrangement according to their preferences and listen to such an arrangement as taped. Objective: comparing with a traditional composition and identifying differences and similarities.

CLASSROOM PRESENTATIONS
OF MUSICAL INSTRUMENTS

The usual practice of bringing musical instruments into the classroom for demonstration is desirable for several reasons. It affords an instant focus of attention, gives the class an opportunity to hear a "live" performer, and presents a real instrument instead of a simulation. There is a good rule to follow in such presentations: The demonstration should be balanced in terms of playing and talking about the instrument, and the emphasis should be on its musical function rather than its mechanics. The "Plan for Trumpet Demonstration" that follows attempts to observe this rule, and to show one way of planning such a demonstration so that the pupils may have an active part in the demonstration. There are many ways to make such a presentation, and a wealth of musical materials is available to vary those suggested. It is important to understand that the "Expected Response" column is simply an attempt to think through the possible pupil responses.

The stated behavioral objective should be checked for pupils' achievement through responses to questions, class discussion, and pupil comments on their observations of musical activities involving trumpets.

Plan for Trumpet Presentation

Behavioral Objective:	Pupil will be able to demonstrate his understanding of the pitch (range), tone quality, and functional musical uses of the trumpet in answering relevant questions.
Materials:	Trumpet, bugle, colored chalk, staff liner
Recordings:	*Trumpeter's Lullaby* (Anderson); *Overture to Rienzi* (Wagner); *Trumpet Voluntary* * (Purcell); *Bugler's Holiday* (Anderson); also examples of jazz trumpet if time allows

Presentation	*Expected Response*
Listen to a bugle call. (Play a few bars of *Reveille*.) How would you react to this?	Get up—move to prepare for breakfast, school.
Why not use a flute for this?	Tone inappropriate.
Inappropriate for what?	Signaling to a large group.
Why?	Tone quality.
Then we've discovered that the bugle here is being used for signals. It is the descendant of cruder instruments such as the ram's horn used to give certain signals. What others can you name?	Conch shell, blowing through cupped hands—other answers.
Let's find out what notes or pitches the bugle can play. (Staff is already on board.) Play all possible notes on bugle. Put on staff.	Ask pupil to circle with red chalk all notes bugle plays.
So the bugle can't play all pitches—just certain ones. Let's look at another instrument, the trumpet. Listen to it and decide whether it plays more notes than the bugle. How is this possible?	Students mention valves or keys. Place term "valves" on board.
Let's have the trumpeter play from the highest to the lowest note on his trumpet. Put notes played on staff.	Ask pupil to circle the highest and lowest notes with blue chalk. Discuss differences with pupils, comparing bugle and trumpet.
What difference does the trumpet's ability to play more notes—we call it a wider "range"—make in its musical use?	Composers can write a wider variety of music; trumpet players can have more scope and variety in what they choose to play.

* *Trumpet Voluntary* was actually composed by Jeremiah Clarke but is usually attributed to Purcell; recordings of the piece are usually listed under his name.

Presentation	*Expected Response*
A trumpet can sound in different ways. Listen! How many different ways did he play?	Listen to trumpeter play faster, slower; softer, louder; crescendo, diminuendo; staccato, legato; muted. List different ways on board.
How would you expect the player or the composer to use these styles in making music?	Class discusses ideas such as echo—softer tone; climax of composition—louder. Add others, having pupils contribute many ideas.
What does the trumpet add to music that no other instrument can add?	This is a summary question.

Other Summary Questions:

1. If you were a composer writing a composition requiring a soprano brass instrument to play a scalewise passage, would you choose bugle or trumpet? Why?

2. Underline the terms in the following list that describe ways the trumpet player can play his instrument or musical things he can do on the trumpet.

staccato	softer	chord	melody
pizzicato	louder	diminuendo	harmony
muted	arpeggio	legato	faster
scales	sharps	louder	flats

3. If you heard *Taps* played on the bugle and then on the trumpet, or vice versa, could you tell which instrument was being played, by sound alone?

Note: If time permits, it would be desirable to include a cornet in the presentation, comparing its tone, range, and musical use with that of the trumpet.

3

Singing

EVERYBODY SING?

Music educators have assumed for many years that singing should be the heart of the music program, and "Everybody sing!" has been a standard rallying cry of the vocal-choral-general music teachers. But does everybody want to sing, need to sing, or are there individual reactions to this musical activity?

The "Everybody sing!" idea probably dates back to the singing school period of American history, the pioneer period of no instruments in churches and few even in secular gathering places. The common instrument of music-making was the voice. Little was available in the way of entertainment; group singing helped. Long before that, singing was one way of spreading news. Today, however, there is entertainment on every hand. One does not have to make his own music. Singing is not heard as a usual group activity in the home; radio and television consume time formerly available for such effort.

That many, but not *all*, adults like or want to sing is fairly evident. Look around in church or other community singing activities. That *all* high school students do not want to sing is indicated by the fact that choral directors do not often, if ever, have their doors battered down by hordes of would-be choristers. That *all* boys do not like or want to sing is painfully apparent from intermediate through the junior high school grades. And there are reluctant singers even in the elementary grades. Why? Perhaps these are some answers.

1. The voice is a personal instrument through which a high degree of communication is achieved. Preschool children sing informally, creatively, and experimentally, and their singing is usually accepted without the strain of correction imposed by parents or other members of the family. But when school experiences begin, the singing experience changes. Now one's voice must begin the process of becoming like other voices—one's tones must sound like other tones—one's song must have the same words as others'. One must please the teacher with his singing; if not, the process of correction and the strain of striving for uniformity are undergone—not always, it would appear, for the sake of a better sound but sometimes for the sake of uniformity. Singing loses its characteristic of being personally expressive—it is enveloped by a group effort. Deviating from the expected norm may result in some type of penalty. (The *"Listen*—don't sing!" philosophy is still encountered at times.)

2. Of all musical experiences or activities, the singing of young children should most qualify as a joyful experience. Yet the processes described above rob it of spontaneity, creativity, and vitality. Here we lose some future singers, undoubtedly.

3. The strain of the chorus-choosing process causes certain children to recognize this as the goal of singing activities, rather than viewing singing as an aspect of musical learning, singing as a purposeful activity with musical learning the goal. If a child rejects the latter goal, he rejects singing participation in many situations.

4. The real emphasis on vocal music tends to be group performance or individual performance for public approbation. Those who reject this goal tend to withdraw from singing activities, either voluntarily or otherwise.

If we want children to achieve satisfactory, self-expressive use of the voice, singing must be put on a basis of its worth as an avenue of musical learning. We must reevaluate our standards of vocal uniformity, group classroom vocal perfection, and choral performance in terms of the individual's perception of such standards.

Pupils must be encouraged to sing, to understand and use their voices, as a means of individual and group musical expression and satisfaction, and as a way to achieve understanding of vocal and choral music. The "Everybody sing" approach as an end in itself is outmoded and unacceptable to today's youth, particularly by the junior high school years. Singing by those who do not want to sing is a hollow activity and one that frustrates both teacher and pupils. In a subject with such a wide range of musical action possibilities, flexibility and choice should be possible.

WORKING WITH THE CHANGING VOICE

The keen, perceptive, educated ear of the teacher is the single most reliable guide to the classification of changing voices. Since such voices come in many sizes and sounds, experience in working with what at first may seem a bewildering complexity of vocal ranges and timbres is the one way to gain skill in understanding such voices and confidence in handling them.

This experience is acquired gradually, and the beginning teacher, working with young voices for the first time, must continually ask himself, "Where (in what range) does this pupil sing most easily, with the most musical and appropriately mature sound? What musical range can be used easily, effectively, and with a sound that satisfies him?" Unfortunately the reverse of this viewpoint is sometimes encountered, and the question then becomes, "Where does my *chorus need* this boy or girl in terms of parts to be sung?" When the latter is a guiding principle, voices are more or less arbitrarily assigned to sections of the choral group or class that need strengthening, and the pupil sings where the music is written, rather than where his voice lies, where he *should* sing. Practices of this sort, and others such as keeping alto-tenors or tenors on higher parts too long, assigning girls to alto-tenor or tenor parts, and failing to check voices frequently and reassign parts as test results indicate, may cause damage to the voice or diminution of interest in singing.

When Does the Voice Change?

1. This varies with individuals, just as physical size varies. There is no fixed time at which boys' voices begin to change. The voice change is part of the total process of maturing.

2. There are indications that American youth matures earlier than we customarily have expected. Look for signs of *beginning* voice change in fifth grade. You may find a few voices in which there are indications of the change onset.

3. Readily observable physical signs which may help identify the boy's changing voice are protruding larynx, prominent nose and jaw, incipient facial hair, prominent wrist and anklebones, change in speaking voice.

Voice change in both boys and girls is part of the maturation process. It is not unduly disturbing to most individuals, but it is a critical period for the singing activities of any school music program, since it is here that we either strengthen the interest in singing, particularly the boys', or, in too many cases, lose pupils as vocal music makers.

How Does the Changing Voice Develop?

1. Sudden versus gradual theories: There is continuing discussion over occurrence of sudden and dramatic voice changes, such as the boy soprano or alto-tenor change to baritone overnight. Such changes may *appear* to be real, but the gradual nature of human growth indicates that this change also is gradual. What *may* show as fairly rapid development is the boy's ability to *articulate* and *control* his new voice. If we are considering the voice change as a total process related to physical growth, the overnight type of change does not seem possible. However, if we are saying that boys suddenly *seem* to be able to sing baritone, this may be possible, just as a child may fall over and over again learning to bike ride, then suddenly seem to learn to balance. The learning has been gradual, however, and the falls were part of it. Close and periodic attention to the changing voice may reveal signs of gradual change otherwise difficult to spot.

2. Range and quality characteristics: The voices of junior high school girls and unchanged-voice boys are usually of treble quality. Baritones are often referred to as changed voices, but actually they are still changing, increasing range both up and down. Boy alto is a middle voice with warm mellow quality. Alto-tenor retains alto quality and is a deeper voice. The voice is maturing downward when the voice is bigger as the singer's range descends.

3. When the boy voice changes, the normal pattern of development is from soprano to alto, to alto-tenor, to baritone, and, in some cases, to bass. Some voices add higher notes to the baritone range in due time, and the boy baritone may become a tenor. This situation should be checked by vocal music teachers; it may be one answer to the lack of tenors in high school choirs. The ease of singing in a particular vocal range is a clue to correct assignment of voice parts.

4. A phenomenon of the changing voice is that a boy may not match a given pitch for starting a song; often he begins lower or higher (sometimes by a fifth) than the pitch sounded. This is possibly due to the fact that although he may hear the pitch correctly, he cannot immediately control his voice so as to produce it vocally. Such boys are too often rejected as being pitch-deficient; many of them will develop into good singers with help and understanding.

The boy baritone does not sound as big, resonant, or mature as a mature baritone. It has a lighter quality and may give the illusion of sounding an octave higher than it really sounds. Likewise, the heavier alto-tenor quality may cause misassignment to the baritone part.

TRYOUTS

The majority of non-professional singers experience a certain degree of fright, or at least nervousness, before and during voice tryouts. This is intensified in the case of adolescents, who are in a highly sensitive stage of development. The beginning of the voice tryout, therefore, should find the teacher putting the pupil at ease, working to help him show his voice to its best advantage, finding what he can do well vocally, and what he has difficulty in doing well, and capitalizing on the strengths of the voice being tested. Teachers may accomplish this, for example, by placing exercises or songs in keys where the pupil seems to be able to perform them easily. Since changing-voice boys sometimes begin singing as much as a fifth above or below the pitch sounded, it helps them if the teacher establishes the song or exercise tonality by sounding the correct tonic triad or playing up and down the scale and then, if a pupil begins singing in a lower or higher key, joining in *his* tonality simply to build his confidence. (We call this "tuning up.") There is always time later to determine whether a pupil has a *pitch* problem or simply a problem of controlling his voice.

Suggestions

1. The student should be tested on a song in a key which is comfortable for him. Perhaps several keys should be tried. In case he starts in another key, the teacher should go to this key. By choosing a key or pitch different from that selected by the teacher, the boy is showing the teacher something about his voice which is relevant to the range in which he can sing. The teacher may test in other keys later in the tryout.

2. The singing material which the pupil is first asked to perform in voice tryouts should be familiar material that he can sing without undue nervousness. *There is a difference between testing a voice and testing reading ability.*

3. Ranges to expect of boys in the changing-voice phase are *approximately* as follows:

Boy bass-baritone

Boy alto-tenor

Boy alto

Boy soprano

The *untrained* boy soprano range is approximately the
same as that of the girl soprano. The *trained* boy soprano
voice has an extremely high range and a very clear, floating
quality. Because of the difference between the untrained
and trained boy soprano voices, no ranges are given.

All these ranges are approximate; the voices are developing continually,
and may be quite limited for periods of time varying in duration. Ranges
develop with practice and confidence.

Signs of Strain in Singing

1. The forward jaw is an indication of tenseness and is usually a sign
   that the boy is singing a part too high for him. Wrinkled brow and
   tense posture sometimes indicate this also.
2. Neck muscles and veins protruding during the singing are a sign of
   strain and tenseness.
3. Complaints about sore throat after singing may mean that the voice
   is being forced and/or artifically produced.
4. Breaking or cracking of the voice while singing may mean that undue
   stress and strain is being placed upon the voice.

All the above may be helped to some degree by stressing correct posture and breathing. Most of all, assignment to the correct singing part
reduces such difficulty.

Following Up on the Development of the Voice

1. Interesting pupils in their individual voices—the idea that each pupil
   has a voice worth examining, checking, and developing—is the best
   single approach. It is important to emphasize the idea that voices are
   interesting to follow in their change and that a boy or girl *can* follow

these changes in his or her own voice. The changing voice charts described by Andrews and Leeder are a means of accomplishing this.[1]

2. Another device that has been successfully used is "Favorite Key Charts." Here the teacher places around the room charts showing each of the key signatures and indicating the position of the home tone in octaves. She then spends some time playing songs in various keys and has the class try them in these keys. Pupils are asked to test their individual singing ranges and decide what key is most comfortable for them, then place their names on the appropriate key chart. This serves a dual purpose: not only do pupils begin testing their own voices but they relate to key signatures and realize their function if they have not already done so. Many singers, of course, do have particular keys in which they sing; it may help to tell pupils this in setting up such a project.

Since the voice-change process is a maturation process, it follows that girls' voices undergo a change. The change in pitch is much more limited than that of the boy's voice but nevertheless deserves careful attention from the teacher. There are very few true alto voices in the junior high school years, but the temptation is great to assign good readers to lower harmony parts because the process of teaching music to a class or chorus is thus expedited. *Range* and *quality* should determine the part a girl sings; in some classes or choruses where there seems to be little real difference in the girl voices as a whole, the best procedure may be to alternate assignments, having a section learn the melody part on one song and the harmony part on another, or sing the higher part in some songs and the lower in others.

OUT-OF-TUNE SINGERS

Children who cannot sing in tune by the time they are in the upper elementary or middle school grades are likely to arrive in the junior high school music class without having shown much improvement. Many teachers think such pupils are lost to the singing program, but this is not necessarily true. To understand the situation, let's take a brief look at the problem in its earlier stages.

Ideas on helping out-of-tune singers (also referred to as pitch-deficient, uncertain, untuned, monotone, tone deaf) have centered on several basic ideas over the years:

1. Inattentiveness to pitch
2. Lack of coordination—voice and ear

[1] Frances M. Andrews and Joseph A. Leeder, *Guiding Junior High School Pupils in Music Experiences* (Englewood Cliffs, N.J.: Prentice-Hall, Inc., 1953), pp. 48–49.

3. Singing range of singing voice (chest quality)
4. Physical defect—throat obstruction or other vocal apparatus defect

To these may be added unfavorable experience with singing at an early stage in a singing experience, prolonged exposure to the idea that the individual concerned cannot sing in tune, and inadequacy of preceding teaching in an earlier grade. (When we are confronted with out-of-tune singers at the college level, usually students who are taking elementary education music courses preparatory to becoming classroom teachers, we have what might be termed "frozen pitch" problems.)

A few approaches to consider when working with students who have real pitch problems follow:

1. *The psychological approach in terms of understanding the problem:* In this approach the teacher attempts to put the student at ease, discover the particular troubles the individual student has, and remedy the situation by means of individual understanding and assistance. This approach cannot be criticized, except that it is trying to remedy a problem which may be only *partly* psychological through what is chiefly a psychological approach. Furthermore, it has a weakness. The teacher is not a psychologist and may never be sure that his approach is the correct one for the individual concerned.

2. The second approach is an input-output approach. The input is a musical tone—a particular pitch—which is recorded on the mind's tonal memory. The output is the *sung* tone. There is an intermediate, internalizing step, however, that is the key to the *sung* tone, the recollection of the *heard* tone. If the process breaks down in the intermediate, internalizing step, the product is certain to be faulty.

What can go wrong between input and output steps? Actually, very little if we thing in terms of discrete steps. But *very* much if we think in terms of interaction among the input, intermediate, and output steps. For example, the out-of-tune singer is nervous, tense, and insecure about the task of singing. This interferes with attentiveness to pitch, and getting a good mental image or recording of the pitch—the input. If the input is poor, the output is poor.

The chief objective in work with out-of-tune singers should be to help them become independent, in-tune singers. The question is how to choose the best means of implementing this objective. Approaches suggested for elementary out-of-tune singers generally have been what is referred to as the "ping-ping" approach—this consists of having the child imitate a tone played on the piano or sung by the teacher. In other words, the child is asked to concentrate on a simple pitch stimulus and respond to it; for very young children the stimulus may take the form of imitating pitch-related sounds, e.g., an animal sound, "bow-wow;" a rising-falling sound, such as a fire siren; or simply a response of "loo-loo" sung back on a given pitch. This is at best a quasi-musical approach. And yet the aim is to get the child to sing in tune, and supposedly to sing a *tune* in tune—not a *pitch* in tune. This last sentence indicates what is wrong with the "ping-ping" approach. The child is not making music. The question raised here is whether or not the child should be asked to concentrate on a minute, exact, specific aspect of the musical process in terms of input-output, or whether it would be better to ask for a gross psychomotor response. Another question involving work with such students is concerned with the fact that they have probably had repeated failures in their attempts to sing. If they fail with a highly delimited task such as singing a single pitch, their ego perception certainly will not improve; it seems unlikely that they will try to improve their singing with anything resembling enthusiasm.

No one would suggest that the techniques often used to help young children learn to sing "in tune" be used for young adolescent out-of-tune singers. Here are some suggestions that are more suitable:

1. Some boys who have been *under*-pitch singers in the elementary school find their in-tune voices during the changing voice period. Occasional private help may be just the boost needed to bring about this result.

2. Remember that remedial help, if given in front of others, may be embarrassing to adolescents and therefore may do more harm than good.

3. In some cases what may really be a vocal production problem may appear to be a pitch problem. If the teacher suspects this, he should concentrate on establishing sound vocal production techniques and temporarily bypass the pitch aspects, hoping these will improve as production improves.

4. Singing a good melody in the right range has helped many singers improve their pitch. Put songs in a suitable range for your adolescent singers. This usually means changing keys.

5. Get your singers to tune to the tonality of each song they sing by first sounding chords, rather than single pitches, to which the singers listen. *Then* sound pitches. Repeated sounding of single pitches teaches pupils *not* to listen attentively. It's impossible to pound pitches into the tonal sense; they must be heard, realized, and translated into a sung, matching sound.

6. Make certain that out-of-tune singers have many opportunities to sing the *melody*. Having to sing a harmonizing part compounds the difficulty.

7. Singing softly in order to hear other singers may be good for in-tune, *certain* singers, but it doesn't help *uncertain* singers gain confidence. *All* singers should be listening while singing, softly or otherwise.

8. Don't expect instant improvement. Changing vocal habits acquired over a six- or seven-year period takes time.

Some Helps for Teaching a Song in Junior High School

1. Give the pitch, or pitches, in octaves for the changed and changing voices. Make sure pupils are on the correct pitch before they begin singing. Thinking—internalizing—the pitch before singing it helps.

2. In working with a part song, stop the piano accompaniment once in a while and have the class continue unaccompanied. This is when you will learn whether or not the class is singing *parts*, or being dominated by the accompaniment.

3. In teaching a new song or reviewing a familiar one, establish the pulse and the rhythmic swing of the music. For example, a song such as "Donkey Riding" is *dead* unless it swings. And don't mistake *speed* for *rhythm*.

4. In having a class imitate rhythmic patterns, have them listen to the pattern more than once. The pupil has to establish both *pulse* and *pattern* in his rhythmic awareness. If a number of patterns are being played simultaneously, make sure there is a strong basic beat underneath the whole.

5. Use rhythmic instruments constructively, not just for the fun of it. Use them to add musical understanding to the song, to emphasize a rhythmic pattern, to develop knowledge of notation. Listen to their timbre; decide where they will have rhythmic impact in an accompaniment.

6. Show the class how to count out the measures of introduction and enter without a signal from you. This helps develop rhythmic awareness of beat, pulse, and meter.

7. It's easy to play the piano so vigorously that the singers are overpowered. The piano should accompany, if it is playing an accompaniment, rather than pull the class along because it is loud.

8. Teach the musical facts *from* the music. If the song has a repeat, a crescendo, or a rest, tell the class what it is, make music with it, use it musically. Better, help pupils *discover* musical meanings.

9. Review what you *think* they have learned. You teach, but they do the learning. Have they learned what you taught, or something else?

10. It's easy to concentrate on the boys and neglect the girls in singing activities. Girls also need help, recognition, attention, and praise.

Suggestions for a Lesson Plan on Teaching a Song

1. State what you plan to teach. Include musical objectives. Be specific, not vague.

   a. Example of specific objective in behavioral terms:
      Compare the sound of the syncopated rhythm pattern in the song to the way it would sound if it were not syncopated:

Describe how syncopation affects the music.

b. Example of vague objective:
"Have the class experience syncopation."

2. List the materials to be used (including such items as songbooks, records, visual aids) and the procedures.

3. Show how the lesson relates to preceding lessons in both objectives and materials. For example, show how the form of the song is similar to or different from that of one or more songs previously studied or one familiar to the class.

4. Indicate the method of presentation, including ways in which the class will participate. Example:

a. Class listens while teacher plays and sings the song.

b. Class reads words rhythmically.

c. Class sings on a neutral syllable, or hums through song.

d. Teacher assigns parts and checks ranges to make sure all voices are compatible with parts.

e. Class sings with words.

f. Class discusses meaning of text.

g. Teacher asks class to locate difficult passages and sing correctly.

h. Class decides on appropriate tempo and sings at that tempo.

i. Class decides on appropriate dynamics.

5. Teacher asks several questions intended to summarize what has been learned and check on the class understanding of the major points covered.

SONGBOOKS

Textbook publishers have conscientiously attempted to produce a product teachers can use effectively. Teams of authors have labored to produce song series that work with pupils. Yet there is sometimes an ingredient too little in evidence in a songbook series, despite the commendable energy, knowledge, and musical learning evidenced by the authors. Perhaps it is a priceless ingredient that can be added only after the songbook is in the hands of the teacher. In any case, the ingredient is *relevance*. It is the factor that speaks to pupils in terms of immediacy and impact on their lives, and it causes them to assign priorities and values in the simplest terms—"This is for me; it says something I want to hear; it is my world, and I want it as part of my scene." It causes them to ask for a certain few songs again and again and to ignore others that have been assigned greater value or priority by musical experts, or it causes pupils to sing the latter songs, when required to do so, as if they *were* ignoring them. A portion of the content of songbooks remains unused by many teachers and their classes, although certain series have been more successful than others.

The criterion that makes a songbook ring true is similar to the one that has caused countless composers to go back to the "real thing," the music of the people, to bring power and relevance to their music. Such composers have used folk music and other music of the people and the times and used it in many forms and guises. Folk music in the songbook series has been successful when not diluted, overly expurgated or prettified in text and arrangement. But even in some instances of the latter, the power and integrity of a song persist and are detected and felt by the singers.

Relevancy is the first criterion to look for, then, in choosing a songbook for junior high school pupils. Remember that it doesn't mean relevancy only in terms of today's music or language idioms. Certain song content is common to many generations of human experience; a pre-adolescent has already acquired much of this common experience. Relevancy is the quality that causes a song to be sung by successive generations of singers in many lands. It will cause a particular song to go through many versions —adapted and resung in taverns and churches and by great assemblies of people, perhaps ending as a hymn or anthem—or to endure despite good or poor singing renditions.

The second criterion is equally important: Do the songs suit the vocal qualities and ranges of those who are to sing them? By now we *do* know where these voices sound best, and the songbook series should accommodate the ranges and the qualities of changing voices. A youngster singing in a range where he cannot sing out with musical satisfaction has a right to be frustrated and to reject the offending materials.

The third criterion relates to harmonizations—does each voice part have a chance to develop some musically powerful singing? Do the boy baritones, for example, have the melody at times? Do those on inner voices have an opportunity to experience harmonic *and* melodic parts that are musically *affective* as well as *effective* in terms of song arranging? Does the music carry along the voice, or must the voice contend with awkward singing lines?

If a songbook can satisfy these three criteria for a teacher, the authors have given him a product that will be valid in real-life terms, and one not likely to be dismissed by pupils as "in-school" music only.

USING SONGBOOKS EFFECTIVELY

Today's youngsters are more highly sophisticated than pupils in any preceding time. They have been exposed to so much music in the form of songs and other compositions, through records, television, and radio, that the contents of the average junior high school songbook may seem unappealing. Perhaps a major reason for such lack of appeal is that mass media materials seem to stress qualities of relevance and immediacy, and we must remember that junior high school youngsters are still living in the present rather than the future; very few of them have a long-range viewpoint.

The constructive and effective use of song textbooks is directly related to the dynamism of the junior high school music teacher. He can make a song come to life, give its words immediacy in terms of meaning and relevance through his own personality and understanding. Whoever writes a song does so out of emotion, the need to tell a story, a desire to set the records straight on some topic, the need to state an idea, a thought, a mood. This lively motivation on the part of the composer (and all songs have composers, although in the case of folksongs the first composer's identity has been lost) is the spark that fires every composer to express himself. Can the teacher manage to interpret the idea of the song and its reason for being so that the class understands and catches the life, the spirit of the song?

The singing of a song without comprehension of its spirit and meaning is nothing more than an exercise in note reading or rote singing. The difference between instrumental music and vocal music is the *text*. How the teacher gets across the message of the composer is really up to him and depends upon his own abilities. If he is an expert pianist, perhaps he can do this by playing songs through and asking the class to follow along as they listen. He may wish to ask the class what their interpretation of the text is; he may wish to sing the song for the class unaccompanied, or accompanied if this is possible. But the musical spirit of the song is the thing, and unless the class catches this, their singing will be an exercise in musical mechanics. After observing many teachers, it is the opinion of the author that nothing really substitutes for the musicality of the teacher; it is this musicality that illumines the text and gets the message to the pupils. Real enthusiasm for and understanding of the song also have much to do with it.

The portion of this chapter that deals with the changing voice makes it clear that these voices simply don't stay put. They are changing in both range and quality. The implication is that to use the songbook effectively the teacher must detect changes needed in the key in which a song is written and accommodate the voices in the class, rather than forcing voices into an uncomfortable range. Teachers should not hesitate to change parts in a song by eliminating a passage that is too high or too low, or substituting one.

With regard to the conveyance of text understanding to the class, it goes almost without saying that there isn't any point in explaining the text of a song such as "Marching to Praetoria," because the meaning of the words is self-evident. On the other hand, pupils sometimes fail to catch the spirit of fun in such a text as "Oh, Susanna." It is true that the words are nonsense words, but they were written in terms of things that had significance in 1840-60. The class will enjoy them more if the teacher explains Foster's work and humor as these qualities are evidenced in his text.

LISTENING TO SINGING

Singers find it difficult to hear and evaluate their own singing, either as individuals or in groups. Yet the singing experience affords an important opportunity for developing musical judgment.

It is suggested that the teacher discuss with pupils appropriate criteria for evaluating their singing and teach them to apply the criteria by first using recordings of professional groups, and then tape-recording their own singing and listening to it. These experiences should transfer to the usual class singing activities. The implication here is not that the singing of a music class should be judged on the same level as that of a professional group, but rather that many of the same criteria apply—such as tone quality, appropriate tempo, dynamic pattern, correct reading of notation, and overall interpretation. Junior high school pupils are intelligent and mature enough to deal with such matters competently.

Another effective means of motivating music classes to improve their singing is to have each class tape-record a few songs and then ask other classes to listen to the taped singing and apply the stated criteria. This aroused great interest in one school where it was tried and proved to be a worthwhile learning experience.

WORK SONGS AND RHYTHMIC FUNCTION

In the teaching of work songs certain confusions have prevailed with regard to the use of accents in the songs as related to the actual work for which the songs were originally intended. Perhaps the following discussion will help.

1. Heavy work songs, such as steel driving songs or certain chanties, made it necessary for a group of workers to pull, haul, tug, pound, or hoist simultaneously. Therefore, everyone moved together—if one member of the gang did not move with the others, the force with which the work was being done was either diminished or totally dis-

rupted. In teaching work songs it is important to emphasize the fact that certain rhythmic motions took place simultaneously. *Identify the accents* in teaching the song.

2. Another category of work songs concerns certain work activities but includes songs that were more ritualistic and may not have *accompanied* work activities. Corn planting songs of the American Indians were not necessarily sung as the corn was planted. It seems difficult to imagine a tribe of Indians dropping a few corn seeds into a hole in the ground, adding a dead fish, covering up the seeds and the fish, and stamping on the ground, all in rhythm! The Indians may have used these as songs sung to the Great Spirit whom they believed governed the growing of the corn, the weather, and other natural events.

3. Other work songs, such as "Cotton Needs Pickin'," were not songs that were always sung as people moved and worked with identical gestures or motions. Picking cotton was a rather individualized activity depending on the amount of cotton to be picked and the size and speed of the worker (children as well as adult men and women participated in the picking). The picking gestures therefore were not necessarily accented. The song may have been sung as people worked to help pass the time, but the accents did not necessarily serve to synchronize the picking motions. A group of workers might have moved down a row rhythmically at a certain pace or tempo, moving to the accents of the song, but not necessarily.

4. In analyzing work songs, it is interesting to ask the children to decide which parts of the body are doing the moving (the "working") in relation to the basic pulse. For example, a class decided that in a capstan chantey the legs and *feet* are the most important rhythmic parts of the body and that this type of chantey is related to a march. In a steel driving song such as "John Henry" the arms are very important, although of course the back and legs are also important. It is possible to stimulate the thinking of children by asking such questions as: "Do work songs with syncopated patterns usually accompany heavy labor?"; "Does a song such as the 'Volga Boat Song' usually have an on-beat or off-beat accent?"

5. Ask the class to discuss reasons why work songs were commonly used fifty or more years ago but are seldom heard today as an accompaniment to labor.

4

Focus on Listening

WAYS TO LISTEN

There are as many ways of listening to music as there are personalities and individuals to listen. Each person brings his own unique experience as a guide to interpreting what he hears. Furthermore, the same individual listens differently at different times, according to a particular mood or state of mind. Sometimes music may evoke an emotional reaction; sometimes a daydreaming, escape fantasy; still again, an intellectual, musical experience. A staggering array of possible pupil attitudes, interests, and experiences confronts the teacher; to this situation one approach in particular seems feasible if he is to function effectively in promoting learning. It is based on the likelihood that the pupil, having found himself in school and in music class, accepts the fact that he should be learning something about the music with which he is presented and wants to learn about it. The teacher's role, then, is to function as a person with broad experience in and knowledge of much music that will be of interest to the pupil in addition to the music he already knows (not *instead* of what he already knows). The teacher's responsibility is to make it easy for the pupil to listen intelligently and enjoyably to music.

FOCUS OF ATTENTION: EXAMPLES OF CONCEPT-CENTERED APPROACH

The pupil should learn from every listening experience and should be able to recognize and articulate a major part of what he has learned in terms of conceptual, musical feedback. This means, of course, that the teacher must be able to plan carefully and in so doing decide on what the learning possibilities of any piece of music are, limit these for any particular class, and decide how they may best be presented so that the pupil will recognize and accept them. Any musical composition of value is made up of countless related dimensions and parts, and while a total effect is important to the listener, he may easily be swamped in an overwhelming complexity of timbres, melodies, harmonies, rhythms, and other musical effects.

With the understanding that classroom presentations should develop from the musical elements and their extensions as discussed previously, and with the further suggestion that presentations be oriented in terms of the General Music Worksheet (p. 67), here are some examples of certain aspects of particular compositions that may become the foci for developing various musical concepts. All compositions, of course, offer a variety of aspects the teacher might use, and it is important to remember that the following are simply examples, any of which could be used for other or additional musical purposes.

1. Ippolitov-Ivanov: "Procession of the Sardar" (*Caucasian Sketches*)

   This excerpt affords an excellent opportunity to direct attention to the rhythmic content of a musical composition. The composer portrays a procession of barbaric tribesmen moving along on spirited horses. He suggests the motion and the character of the participants through choice of rhythmic patterns and instruments.

   Direct the attention of pupils to the lively rhythmic pattern underlying the melody. Have them experiment with this pattern, trying various rhythm instruments until they arrive at appropriate choices. Listen to the music and ask whether the instruments give the effect of playing simultaneously or one after the other; ask whether this has an effect on ideas of movement and national characteristics of music.

2. Beethoven: "Turkish March" (*Ruins of Athens*)

   This may be used as an example of loudness (dynamics) employed by the composer to convey the idea of spatial movement. Focus the attention of the class on the importance of the *loudness* changes. Have them decide on the correct setting of a metronome for this composition; then direct their attention to the *steady* tempo. If the *tempo* does not change, what *does* reflect the approach and departure of these spirited marchers? Develop discussion leading to understanding of dynamic values: pp, ff, pp.

3. Copland: *Lincoln Portrait*

The composer uses a folk song, "Springfield Mountain," and a Foster Song, "Camptown Races" to suggest various facets of Lincoln's personality and the time in which he lived.

Just as utilitarian instruments of the people (such as early forms of the horn) may develop into true musical instruments, the simple songs of the people are often used by composers in larger forms of music. Such compositions as *Lincoln Portrait* help pupils understand how the whole jigsaw of music and music-making fits together. Emphasize the relationship between folk music and larger musical works.

4. a) Purcell: "Trumpet Voluntary"

   b) Anderson: "Trumpeter's Lullaby"

The concept of the performer's style may be developed from the use of these two examples of trumpet playing.

Focus attention of pupils on comparing tone quality, phrasing, dynamics, and other aspects of interpretation. Point out how the player's style may be affected by the music he is playing.

5. Bizet: "Carillon" (*L'Arlesienne Suite No. 1*)

Here we have an object (bells or chimes) imitated by the orchestra. Without resorting to the use of bells, the composer creates the effect of the carillon through a repeated pattern of sharply accented notes.

The area of emphasis here is the way in which the composer employs musical means to create the effect or illusion of ringing bells. What musical elements or combination of elements cause the illusion? Ask the class to listen to the entire composition: does the bell-like figure ever stop?

6. Schubert: "The Erlking" ("Der Erlkönig")

This, one of the greatest of all art songs, has so many teaching possibilities for developing musical understanding and enjoyment that one has difficulty choosing. The tremendous piano accompaniment creates an atmosphere of tension and drama, suggesting the galloping of the horse and the rushing of the wind. The four voices of the singer (story teller, father, child, Erlking) and the singer's skill in dramatizing these parts through the vocal music will interest the pupils. Pupils may be able to imagine the drama from an outline of the story, listening to the four voices as the singer changes from one to another, and also from identifying key words in the German. The story teller opens the song; the first words of the father are "My son . . . ;" the first words of the Erlking are "Thou dearest boy . . ."

Since the language barrier is one that puzzles teachers, try placing some of the German key words on the chalkboard:

Narrator: "Wer reitet" (Who rides)

Father: "Mein Sohn . . ." (my son)

Child: "Der Erlkönig, Vater" (The Erlking, Father)

Father: "Mein Sohn . . ." (my son)

Erlking: "Du liebes Kind . . ." (Thou dearest boy)

Point to these key words as they are sung.

The basic musical concepts to be developed include importance of accompaniment in art songs, vocal skill of singer through ability to vary voice, rhythmic drive of song, significance of triplet figure in accompaniment.

7. Respighi: *The Pines of Rome*

In the section entitled "The Pines Near a Catacomb" the composer establishes contact with the past through the use of muted strings and horns and the fragment of an old religious chant. Here the class may find it interesting to discuss this fragment, what it represents, why the composer used it.

In the section entitled "Janiculum" the composer depicts a moonlit scene with a nightingale singing. Instead of using instrumental means to convey the song of the nightingale (flute or clarinet, for example), a recorded nightingale is heard. A basic idea to be conveyed to pupils is that of *realism* in music. Also interesting to discuss may be the composer's choice of accompaniment for the nightingale's song.

8. Mozart: *Horn Concerto No. 3 in E Flat,* Third Movement

This movement is a lively rondo. Most junior high school pupils have a general idea of form through their observations of people, furniture, houses, pictures, and so forth. Some, but not all, pupils have an idea of song form from their elementary experiences with song material.

This rondo form is quite obvious: A-B-A-C-A. The pupils must be able to identify A so they will spot it when it recurs. They may also look for the bridge or transitional passages to and from the B and C themes. (It may make more sense to some pupils to use 1-2-1-3-1 instead of A-B-A-C-A.)

The meaning of the term "rondo" seems obvious to most adults and to many pupils. Others may be helped to understand it through discussion or a device such as a poem:

A The lonely wind blows from the hill

B And chills the garden rose.

A The lonely wind blows from the hill

C And brings the drifting snows.

A The lonely wind blows from the hill.

For those who are more literal-minded, an example such as a three-decker sandwich has been used effectively. (Bread, meat, bread, cheese, bread.)

The basic musical concept to be developed is that of form in music.

9. Moussorgsky-Ravel: "Bydlo" (*Pictures at an Exhibition*)

The music suggests the ponderous motion of a Polish oxcart, described by use of rhythm and dynamics.

Compare the tempo and lumbering movement of this music to the neat, snappy movement of Beethoven's marchers in the "Turkish March."

Some musical ideas that may be developed are tempo, choice of instruments to depict cart, lumbering rhythmic motion of vehicle as it moves along.

10. Puccini: Act III, *Tosca* (Opening)

Here the composer is setting a scene. The music seems to begin in an "It was a day like any day . . ." manner. The young shepherd drives his flock through the streets and sings his song of hope and despair. Rome begins to awaken. The bells of the many churches and the gradual change in the mood of the orchestra lead us to the inevitable conclusion that for someone this is an ill-fated day.

The basic musical concept to be developed has to do with opera. An integral part of the composer's ability to write an opera lies in his musical ability to set a scene. Here the composer uses the church bells in their various pitches, rhythmic patterns, and timbres against the orchestral sound of melody, harmony, and instrumentation.

11. Grofé: "Cloudburst" (*Grand Canyon Suite*)

Many composers have written musical descriptions of storms. Pupils may be interested in considering what instruments *they* would choose to create a storm effect in music. Ask pupils to listen to "Cloudburst" and list the instruments used by the composer. Then ask them to listen again, considering the way in which he has players *use* their instruments.

The areas of musical emphasis to be considered here pertain to performing techniques and orchestration.

Basic Principles for Making a Listening Study Guide

1. Remember that the Study Guide is a *learning* rather than a testing instrument, an organized information and knowledge sheet intended to develop understanding of the music being heard and to lead to growing discrimination in music.

2. Prior to making the Study Guide, gather extensive information on the composition and its composer. Study it to determine what aspects are to be stressed in the presentation; choose items for the Guide on this basis. Try to include such items as musical themes, rhythm patterns, musical symbols, instruments or voices, dynamic patterns, and others appearing on the Chart (p. 27).

3. Be sure the Study Guide contains, in concise form, all the information pupils are to learn. Organize the information in such a way that the pupil can easily recognize, retrieve, and apply it to the music as he listens. Try it several times before using it in class; make sure it is not too complicated.

4. As a means of organization, use multiple choice, brief completion, matching, and true-false items. Each of these should be structured so as to provide a means of reaction to the music that can be readily and rapidly recognized and indicated by the pupil.

5. Pace the Study Guide so the pupil can work out answers while listening to the composition, with an additional period of time for checking and review if needed. Avoid the mistake of making a Study Guide so involved that it interferes with and distracts from the listening experience. The Guide should increase the significance of listening and provide a focus of attention.

6. Stress the problem-solving aspects of listening, the *hows* and *whys* that reveal reasons for musical characteristics of a composition, rather than the *whats* that provide factual answers. ("*How* did the composer suggest the rising wind?" "*Why* did the composer use a trombone glissando?" "The composer uses brass instruments to play the fanfare. If he had used stringed instruments, would the volume have been louder, softer, or the same?")

7. Arrange the Study Guide sequentially, so that each piece of information leads to the next, reveals additional knowledge, or is cumulative in reference to several points.

8. a)   Include an item in each Study Guide that allows the pupil to express his *own* individual feelings about, interpretation of, or reaction *to*, the music. Allow room for imagination! Example:

   1)   The music made me feel (describe your feelings about the music):

   _____

   2)   The music reminded me of _____

   _____

   3)   When the composer wrote this music, I believe he was thinking about _____

   b)   Pupils also need room to relate and apply new musical information to different musical problems. Questions such as the following are of interest to them: In *Pictures at an Exhibition* the composer uses the "Promenade" theme to depict people walking. If an arranger adapted this theme to describe people *running* from a rainstorm, how might he change it?

9. When listening, call out items by number or letter in such a way that they will be easily identified for purposes of discussion, or for collating the listening with completing the Study Guide (e.g., "Item No. 4 coming up now!").

10. Keep pupils informed as to whether or not they are performing well in working out the items on study guides. Collect the guide sheets and check them, at least occasionally, and provide feedback as to progress.

Example of a Listening Study Guide Using Matching Items

THE MOLDAU (VLTAVA—THE RIVER)

Bedřich Smetana

How would you like to follow a river back to the very place it began, then journey along with it until it meets the sea? One composer envisioned many different sights that might appear along its banks when he wrote a musical version of a river's journey in his country Bohemia (now Czechoslovakia). This composer has been called a nationalist because his music reflects the beauty of his native land.

What makes a river? How does it begin? This river, the Moldau, begins when two springs, a noisy and a quiet one, join and start a journey that leads eventually to the sea. How do you think the composer describes each spring, their forming into a brook and river, and the scenes through which the river passes?

Before each scene listed in Column I, place the letter indicating the musical means by which the composer describes the scene, choosing from the musical clues in Column II below.

If you hear anything that makes the music interesting *in addition to* the items listed, please feel free to add it after (h) or (i).

I		II
_____ Broadening of the brooklet into a river (Song of the River)	a)	Happy dance tune, heavy accents, bagpipe drone effect
_____ Forest and hunting scene	b)	Ghostly music, soft, staccato; horns in harmony
_____ Village Wedding		
_____ Moonlight scene	c)	Trumpet and horn hunting calls, galloping rhythm
_____ Old Castle		
_____ Rapids of St. John	d)	Broad singing melody, violins, oboes
_____ Triumphant Theme (Song of the River)	e)	High sustained violin tones with rippling accompaniment; soft
	f)	Big chords, big melody, building to climax, then dying away
	g)	Brass, woodwinds, strings. percussion; listen for cymbals
	h)	
	i)	

Describe one river scene you believe the composer might have added or substituted for one of the scenes he did use. Tell how you would have made your scene sound. (Use other side of paper if necessary.)

USING QUESTIONS TO DISCOVER MUSICAL ANSWERS

The process of helping youngsters discover answers is one that keeps them interested and motivated because in the hands of an adept teacher pupils *do* discover the right answers and thus receive recognition, praise, and reinforcement. This, on the surface, is not necessarily an efficient process, and it takes longer than does presenting information in a neat, logical package. The neat, logical package approach is appropriate at times, of course. It is also often dry and lacking in appeal.

Amahl and the Night Visitors, an opera in one act by Gian-Carlo Menotti, is an example of a musical work that has unlimited potential for pupil discovery of what is going on in the music and why the composer chose certain musical techniques in creating his opera.*

The teacher in presenting this opera should certainly try to convey to the class a working concept of what an opera is. To many of the un-initiated, opera is a jumble of singing and instrumental sounds, with some of the singing being so stylized and foreign to the experience of the listener that it is funny. Explaining that opera is a great art form is not going to convey the concept of a living, significant work. Illustrating with everyday examples is a better approach: try experimenting by saying something to a member of the class who will enter into the spirit of the experiment. Ask him to respond, then *sing* the same dialogue or a fol-low-up of the original dialogue. Make it recitative, and *let them laugh!* Then explain the purpose of recitative, and bridge from there to aria, and so on. Keep hitting the point that the sung message is more dramatic and attention-getting and is musical language rather than just spoken lan-guage. This is an imaginative approach, though, and the teacher who uses it must have a light touch with one hand and keep control with the other.

In the discovery approach we are trying to emphasize the *Why* and *How* of a musical process or product. It's difficult to answer *Why* and *How* questions with facts; they elicit problem-solving, concept-based answers, while *Who* and *What* questions are terminal. Example: "Who composed this opera?" "Gian-Carlo Menotti." Now consider: "Why did the composer choose this particular story as the text of his opera?" "Because it was a story he and his brother had loved when they were children, and he

* The teaching material on *Amahl,* from which the material on these pages has been adapted, was originally developed by the author and Virginia Croft, then a junior high school general music teacher.

remembered it at the time he was looking for a story or theme for an opera he was to compose."

The nineteen illustratory questions that follow are intended to stimulate the teacher's thinking and serve as examples. Not all could be used in any one class period, of course. And answers are not given; it is suggested that the teacher listen to *Amahl* and decide how the answers develop from the music. Use these examples in whatever way they will serve to stimulate the interest of the class in discovering the nature of the composer's musical action. The beauty of the music will speak better to the listeners through such revelation, and they will be developing musical understanding.

AMAHL AND THE NIGHT VISITORS
Gian-Carlo Menotti

Opening Scene

The opening scene of this opera depicts an early evening sky, very clear, with many stars shining brightly. The Christmas or Eastern star is very prominent. Amahl, a young boy, is sitting outside his small cottage home playing on his shepherd's pipe; we know he is lame since his homemade crutch is beside him. His mother is inside the house, and through the open door we see a small fire burning and a dimly-lit, poorly-furnished room. The action in this opening scene is between Amahl and his mother—she wants him to come into the house, and he wants to stay out longer watching the sky, especially the fantastically bright star, and playing his shepherd's pipe. Amahl is a dreamer, given to making up tall tales, and his mother has learned to distrust what he reports to her. This is important to remember because several of the actions in the opera hinge upon it.

The voices of the singers and the orchestra reflect the action, enhance it, and make it more significant. In studying Amahl, we are going to explore how the composer accomplishes this. The following questions are pointed toward helping the pupils discover the musical action, in voices and orchestra, that makes the plot more significant.

1. How does the music reflect the clear, dark evening sky? Does the composer use heavy chords played by brasses, for example, or does he use lighter melodies and instruments? Is the music smooth and flowing (legato), or detached and abrupt (staccato)?

2. The composer might have chosen to use flute or clarinet, rather than oboe, to represent Amahl's shepherd's pipe. For what reason may he have decided to use the oboe?

3. In choosing the best melodic pattern for Amahl's mother to use in calling to him, which of the following did the composer choose?

———   ———   ———

———

———   ———   ———

Which of the following melodic patterns did the composer use for Amahl's answer to his mother?

             ————   ————

          ————

———— ————   ————   ————

4. Amahl is lame. He limps as he walks. How does the music show this?
5. How does Amahl's voice tell you that he is a boy and not a grown man?
6. Which first tells you that the mother has lost her patience with Amahl, her singing or the orchestra's playing? How does the composer accomplish this?
7. What is the chief role of the orchestra during the argument as tension mounts between Amahl and his mother? Does it dominate or accent?
8. Which is more important in an opera, the role of the singers or the role of the orchestra?
9. Which of the following do you hear in this scene: voices in harmony, a chorus, solo voices, band, string quartet?

Entry of the Kings Scene

10. When we first hear the procession coming from the distance, does it sound like an oriental procession or like a procession we might see going down the streets in our own town?
11. In the dialogue between Amahl and his mother when they are arguing about what Amahl sees outside the door, how does the orchestra describe the movements of Amahl?
12. When the Kings come into the cottage, is this a colorful procession? How does the composer introduce this? How does he describe it musically?
13. Why doesn't the composer herald the entry of the Kings with trumpets and the other brass instruments which are traditionally used to signal the entrance of important persons?
14. How does the composer show us that Kasper is deaf?
15. How does the composer use silence rather than music to heighten the suspense as Kasper reveals the contents of the third drawer? What musical symbol would show this?
16. Listen to the voices of the Three Kings and tell how each suits the temperament of the particular King. Which King, do you think, is leader of the expedition?
17. In singing a carol such as "We Three Kings" how would you choose a voice from your own classroom to sing the part of each King? Listen to some voices and cast the parts of the Kings by describing the voices.
18. Listen to the "Shepherds' Chorus" and decide how the voices and music describe the simple country people who come to greet the Kings.
19. The composer has said that as a child King Melchior was his favorite King, and Kasper was his brother's. Which King sings a song that is very appealing to children?

CONCEPT-DIRECTED QUESTIONS ON PETER AND THE WOLF

Peter and the Wolf is a musical composition many pupils have already heard by junior high school years. Because they know its music, the teacher is in a favorable position to help pupils consider it in terms of understanding the use of such musical devices as instruments, melody, harmony, and rhythmic effects. The following Study Guide considers some basic musical information from which concepts may develop.

Example of a Listening Study Guide Using Concept-Directed Questions

PETER AND THE WOLF

Sergei Prokofiev

Discussion Questions Leading to Musical Learning

1. Peter, who is played by the _____

   (name instruments or group) is a lively, happy boy. How does his music

   tell you this? _____

   _____

2. When the composer wrote the "cat climbing the tree" music, why didn't he

   have the clarinet play right up the scale? _____

   _____

   Do you think the cat goes right to the top of the tree and stays there? How

   do you know? (Give a reason for your opinion.) _____

   _____

   _____

3. What instrument represents the hunters' shooting? Could other instruments

   have been used for this? If so, which? _____

   _____

How would rifle shots sound to a small boy—loud or soft? _____

_____

4. When lassoing the wolf, does Peter drop the lasso straight down? _____

_____

How does the music describe the lassoing? _____

_____

5. Tell some of the ways Grandfather's tune is different from Peter's. _____

_____

_____

6. If you wanted a flute to show that the bird was frightened, what might the composer have the player do to indicate this? _____

_____

Would the hunters, as they would seem to Peter, be represented by a bigger or a smaller sound? _____

7. If the composer had been portraying Peter as a high school senior instead of a small boy, what instrument might he have chosen to represent him?

_____

_____

USING A GENERAL MUSIC WORKSHEET

Many teachers believe that some type of response sheet or other written record of musical learning experience is a valuable reinforcement. Since it is generally accepted that reinforcement is a necessary instructional technique, this alone would justify the time and effort required of the teacher to develop such materials. It is also important, however, that pupils have some kind of cumulative, visual record of their musical activities, particularly in the case of general music class where the content is not covered by one, or even several, textbooks.

GENERAL MUSIC WORKSHEET

	Instrument(s), Including Singing Voices	Composer; Arranger — Style, Period, Emphasis on Major Contributions to Music	Performer(s) — Emphasis on Style, Technique, Musicianship, Interpretation
Pitch — Higher – Lower, Melody, Harmony			
Duration — Longer – Shorter, Faster – Slower, Tempo, Meter, Rhythm, Pulse, Accent, Beat			
Loudness — Louder – Softer, Volume, Dynamics, Stress			
Timbre — Tone color, Tone quality, Texture			
Form — Organization: Repetition, Contrast, Variety, Balance			

Title of Composition _____

Composer _____

Performer _____

Period Lived _____

Major Contribution to Music _____

The General Music Worksheet illustrated is organized in terms of a matrix resulting in a number of "learning blocks," each of which deals with the extension of a musical element into composed music. For example, "pitch," in the case of a Bach fugue, would extend into "Bach—polyphonic" in the "composer" learning block, with appropriate comments in other blocks as teacher and class think relevant and applicable. Certain Bach fugues elicit tremendous *crescendi* and *decrescendi* from the performer(s), whether on organ or orchestra; these would be noted in the "loudness" or "performer" matrix block. The teacher, however, might wish to use only two or three of the blocks for a particular learning episode summary. The time available for general music classes seldom permits an exhaustive analysis of any one composition.

The Worksheet matrix may also be used for a record of musical learning resulting from songs learned by the class, since we assume that singing is more than a psychomotor activity. Much can be learned or reinforced by the actual application of musical techniques—dynamics, for example—in singing. One of the great weaknesses of music education is that classes are often so busy singing that they stop short of the musical learning that should be a concomitant development.

The thoughtful use of the General Music Worksheet matrix, in whatever manner the teacher believes best, can be a vitalizing factor in providing continuity and reinforcement for musical growth.

COMPOSERS: WHAT ABOUT THEIR IMAGE?

Try talking with your pupils on the subject of composers, their personalities, characters, and lives in general. Their impressions are usually fragmentary, consisting of isolated and not always correct bits and pieces which are dull and have little to do with the great one's music. Adults may be interested in the information that Bach had twenty children, that Handel practiced stealthily in the attic by candlelight, and that Foster had serious problems and ended up in Bellevue, but these certainly do not convey the real image of what a composer is and does. In today's world composers are often average human beings having much the same problems as other people, although they experience somewhat more dramatic successes and failures.

The essence of what should be learned about a composer centers on what his life had to do with the music he composed and how the time and place in which he lived influenced his creative musical life. The fact that Beethoven grew deaf is not as important as the fact that he could still hear in his mind the music he continued to create and perform; this is a triumph of the human spirit over a physical handicap.

Teachers should try to develop the understanding that composers live in every period, that many composers live and work today. Why not include the lives and works of contemporary composers? It helps pupils understand that people compose music today; it avoids the impression that all composers are dead.

In teaching young people about composers, try to help them see that each composer was an individual much like other human beings, and make him as believable as possible. Each teacher will find his own way of doing this, of course, but for the sake of illustration, a short example follows. Let's assume that it might interest a seventh grade class.

BEETHOVEN: MUSICIAN AND REBEL

No one today thinks of Beethoven as other than a grown-up composer of great music. Yet one of his neighbors said, long after he was famous, "I can still see him, a tiny boy standing on a little footstool, in front of the clavier and weeping." [1]

Why? Because his father saw in his talented son chiefly a means of making money, so he forced the little boy to practice many long hours and made him play concert after concert.

You might think that Beethoven would grow up hating music! But he didn't. Instead, he grew up liking music but hating all forms of tyranny. This resentment of too strict control eventually included rebellion against the confining rules that governed the writing of music. Beethoven broke some of these rules, but he *made other, better rules to take their place.* This is important to remember.

You could never call Beethoven a musical copycat. The music of Haydn and Mozart was too tame for him. He wrote music that was free to sound as *he,* Beethoven, wanted it to sound. If he felt like putting a thunderstorm into a symphony he did, and the orchestra reverberated with very loud chords. If he felt sad, he wrote music that expressed great sorrow, such as the "Funeral March" in his great *Eroica Symphony, No. 3.* If he felt happy, he wrote a gay "Scherzo," or a funny piece about someone who lost a penny and in trying to retrieve it found that it kept rolling back into a crack in the walk in an infuriating fashion! He wrote about nature, about people, about world events in his music, and this music we call descriptive because it tells us something, or it follows a program of events that happen in the music.

The music of Beethoven was different in dynamics, in tempo, in rhythm, and in form from any music that had been written. For instance, Haydn threw in only *one* loud chord in his *Surprise Symphony,* but Beethoven threw in great blockbusters of chords when he wanted to—at the end of a symphony, for example. (He really shook up his audiences!) When he wrote the music that described one story, the "Egmont Overture," he said that he wrote the music

---

[1] Lillian Baldwin, *A Listener's Anthology of Music,* Vol. I (Morristown, New Jersey: Silver Burdett Company, 1948). Copyright, 1948 by Lillian Baldwin, p. 128. Reprinted by permission.

after reading the play and then gave out his reaction in music. About this music one person wrote, "It begins with a long, loud tone, every instrument of the orchestra uniting, as did every voice is the Netherlands, in the common cry of suffering." [2]

Beethoven wrote what is called "romantic" music. But this does not mean "romantic" in the sense of a love affair—it means that he expressed individual and unique feelings in a style of music that was his own. Now discuss this: Did Haydn write romantic music?

Beethoven freed music from many rules and regulations. He put his own feelings into his music, but even more he expressed the feelings of mankind. We still value his work because he wrote music for all of us to hear, feel, and enjoy. It has endured and been remembered and played year after year. This is the great test!

Agree or Disagree with These Statements:

_____   Beethoven would have done a good job if he had been asked to write music for a recording to be called "Music to Agree By."

_____   Beethoven's music was better than, but the same type as, Haydn's.

_____   Beethoven's music was pretty, but it didn't say much.

_____   Romantic music is highly patterned and very formal.

_____   If you hear music that has very soft and very loud passages, with heavily accented chords, chances are it was written by Bach or Haydn but not by Beethoven.

_____   Beethoven's audiences were not surprised to hear a scherzo in one of his symphonies.

_____   Beethoven's music influenced that of other composers.

[2] Baldwin, *A Listener's Anthology*, p. 168.

5

Creativity
in General Music

WHY MORE CREATIVITY IN MUSIC CLASS?

Music is an expressive art, a medium of communication, and an avenue to self-realization and fulfillment. Or *has* it been, in public schools? Much emphasis has been put on music as a group activity; more needs to be placed on the individual, creative aspects of the subject. There is clear evidence to support this belief: the springing up of informal music groups unsponsored by the school, groups made up of youngsters who are expressing themselves by being creative in their own way, regardless of school standards and values. Much emphasis has been placed on group activity in the schools, of course, but on rather strictly regimented groups where musical choice of content and action is concerned. More needs to be placed on the individual, creative aspects of the art. Why has this been lacking in the past? Why has music, an art and a discipline which should be one of the most creatively learned of all subjects, been in practice one of the least creatively taught? Answers to such questions may include the following:

1. Emphasis on group learning. This begins in the earliest grades, where emphasis is on getting all children to sing the same unison notes in chorus. Often more attention is given to the correctness of the notational rendition than to the musical spirit of the song. The song, in other words, may be lost in the notes. Yet it is known that many artist singers deviate in one way or another and to some degree from the score as printed. (The values of some group performance may be more social by far than creative *or* musical.)

2. A similar approach prevails in the teaching of instrumental music. The mode is group instruction, with priority on acquiring skill in control of a musical instrument. Group instruction precludes emphasis on realization of a major reason for learning to play an instrument—self-expression through music. And although it is true that a skilled musical group is able to perform music expressively, it is a second-hand expression—relayed through the conductor's interpretation and perception.

3. Emphasis on large ensemble public performance. No degree of *individual* expression is possible in a large group—conformity to the group's expression is the *sine qua non*.

4. Even in individual vocal or instrumental instruction, constraint is provided in the form of a model or exemplar, with the expectation that the pupil will imitate. Seldom are differing models provided and the pupil encouraged to compare, analyze, and work toward developing the behavioral mode that most suits his individuality—physical and otherwise.

5. Emphasis in the study of music literature—often referred to as appreciation class—is on the end product, rather than on the process of the composer in creating his music.

All of this may be defended, of course, by saying that pupils must learn fundamentals of technique, music reading, and basic knowledge of an existing body of musical literature. Too often, however, the process never goes beyond this. What, then, needs to be done to encourage creativity in the musical learning process? What is a constructive approach to the development of creativity in music classes? Obviously, more emphasis on the role of the individual. Yet general music classes are notoriously large, by common report often larger than classes in other subject areas. How can we work creatively with individuals in large groups?

A CREATIVE APPROACH

First, it may be assumed for our purposes that all boys and girls are both creative and musical to a greater or lesser degree. The realization that one is creative, even to a limited extent, is a means of self-fulfillment and self-realization, and the teacher has an obligation to reveal this to the pupil. The pupil who is *highly* creative may make great and original contributions to the arts, humanities, or sciences; here, too, the teacher has an obligation.

Second, the teacher needs an understanding of the creative individual. Highly creative children often challenge a teacher's patience, ingenuity, flexibility, and resourcefulness. They may not conform to the teacher's expectation of the normally well-behaved, cooperative pupil. They have been characterized as original thinkers, possessing imagination, a sense of humor that may cause them to laugh at disconcerting times when the teacher is not expecting laughter, and a general tendency to challenge traditional procedures and look for different ways of doing things. They perceive relationships differently than do less creative children. While not necessarily in the highest range of intellectual giftedness, they are at least normally intelligent. The creative individual, evidently, is one who hears a different sound, sees a different color or form, perceives a different pattern of relationships or operations than do his fellows. This is his gift, his unique quality, and also the substance of his potential. It is not always well received or understood, so it becomes, too often, his burden and frustration. Teachers—even parents at times—find it difficult to accept the child who is different in his perceptions and behavior; it is unfortunate when the difference becomes a threat to adult security. For example, a creative child may question the value of learning all the key signatures once he understands the structural arrangement of the diatonic scale. Some teachers will see this as a challenge to authority; a wise teacher will accept such questions as a groping for information, as honest inquiry, and will point out that many different scales exist. A creative child may learn from experimenting with the pentatonic scale and other scales and from devising original scales in different interval arrangements. This will call for some teacher help, but it is constructive where the encouragement of creativity is concerned and is an example of supporting, rather than repressing, its development.

Third, there is more potential for fostering individual activities in music class than is usually supposed. The jumble of noise from a variety of activities carried on simultaneously bothers the teacher more than the pupils, and while it calls for steady nerves and a stable disposition to have one group singing, another listening with headsets, a third experimenting with the piano, and a youngster making up scales on bell blocks, it can be done. The whole difficulty may be in the level and mix of sounds the teacher can accommodate, since music class produces more decibels than do other subjects, and the music educator is more sensitively attuned to sound than other teachers.

Fourth, the teacher must be willing to follow the lead a creative individual may indicate, to accept unusual and original approaches and ideas about musical activities. The creative process is usually an exploring, problem-solving process, but both problem and solution may be so unusual that neither teacher or pupil may be aware of definition or boundaries. The teacher must also be proficient in suggesting challenging questions that arouse curiosity, the "What if . . ." type of question. Tolerance of both mistakes and the pursuit of seemingly fruitless leads are needed when developing creativity—mistakes are part of creative approaches, and unusual, often accidental, approaches are characteristic of many discoveries.

IMPLICATIONS FOR MUSIC EDUCATION

Music education will not be able to explore its potential as a creative, prime educative force until it effectively frees itself from the constraints of performing organizations and accepts other behavioral modes *by releasing its pupils to fulfill themselves, instead of the public, through music.* The creative *individual* experiences and realizes himself not as a plurality, but as a unique human being; his viewpoint is that "*I* hear music, *I* play music, *I* compose music—*I*, an individual. Not a single musical composition has been written by an ensemble. No one has ever commissioned a committee to create a composition. So free *me* to realize music as an individual. Chances are I'll perform my role as a group member just as effectively, too. It's even possible that I'll function better, because I'll be accepted as an individual with musical ideas of my own to bring to the group. Help me be more than a 'warm body' member!"

EXERCISES IN CREATIVITY

Research and writing on creativity indicate that creative people are well versed and knowledgeable in their fields of endeavor rather than uninformed, uninstructed, and naive. They look at things differently; their ideas conjoin in an atypical manner. If schools are to foster creativity, such divergent thinking is to be encouraged. Here are a few exercises that may foster some creative musical thinking. Turn your classes loose on them and see if you identify some creative ability.

1. Here are three musical instruments, a tympani (tympanum), a trombone, and a tambourine. If you showed them to visitors from a primitive tribe who had never seen or heard these instruments before, what

do you think they would be most likely to decide on as their probable uses, musical or otherwise?

2. Using the same instruments, discover how many different tone qualities you can get by playing them conventionally or otherwise.

3. Using any non-verbal means you can think of, describe the tone quality of a bassoon.

4. Make up a sentence that expresses anger. Now make up a) a melody to express it, and b) a non-melodic, rhythmic expression of the sentence. Can it be done so that the meaning of the sentence is communicated?

5. Make up an original scale which you believe can be used for singing and playing original tunes. When you are fairly sure you have a satisfactory scale, tell the class the reasons you think it will work.

6. Conduct an imaginary interview with J. S. Bach to get his reactions to The Swingle Singers records and the Peter Schickele records (P.D.Q. Bach and others).

7. Write a newspaper advertisement explaining the advantages of the newly-invented pianoforte over the harpsichord.

8. While one of your classmates improvises a melody on a classroom instrument, try making up an accompaniment on another instrument.

6

Classroom
and Pupil Management

WHAT ARE THEY LIKE?

Junior high school pupils are like many other human beings—studies in contradiction, but to a greater extent than most adults. They are energetic and dynamic when motivated and interested, lazy, and indifferent when bored. They are considerate, compassionate, and thoughtful when in sympathy with the other person or persons with whom they are involved. Or, they are rude, thoughtless, and defiant when out of sympathy with what they do not understand or consider important. They are great fighters for a cause they believe to be worth supporting, but they can oppose an unfair situation, or one they believe to be unfair, relentlessly. They can be reasoned with if approached at the right time and in the right way. They have their emotional ups and downs like the rest of the world, but because they are still growing up, these are more extreme and less controlled. They can learn fast and well, carry off tremendously difficult projects, plan, work, persevere, endure and prevail despite formidable obstacles. Much seems to depend on their attitude toward the adults who teach and supervise them. This, of course, makes the teacher's role extremely critical. The teacher has to accept, tolerate, accommodate, reinforce, support, and encourage, while at the same time being firm, consistent, and even-tempered in order to provide a secure frame of reference. The great thing about junior high school youngsters is that they *are* growing and developing, rather than fixed. They are amenable to change, and they are eminently teachable. But they have little respect for the teacher whose efforts do not deserve respect—you just can't fool them.

However much is written about these youngsters in books on adolescent psychology (and reading such material is to be encouraged), the preceding comments sum up their wonderful characteristics. The teachers who work with them will always be challenged, and should find the challenge rewarding.

ESTABLISHING PUPIL CONTROL

In the final analysis each pupil controls his own behavior, with reinforcing assistance from the teacher. This "reinforcing assistance" is a frame of reference established by pupils and teacher, the parameters of which are based on one principle, that of pupil freedom, as long as this does not have a negative, or trespassing, effect on the constructive activities of other individuals and the class as a whole. The degree of individual freedom varies in relation to a) the number of members in the class, and b) the mode of a particular musical activity that engages the attention of the class.

With this general principle established, the next step is to let pupils know what behavior is expected. This can be done on an informative basis by announcing classroom ground rules. The fewer specific *don'ts,* the better; once announced, these must be enforced. There are always a few pupils who by chance or design instigate "test cases." Pupils can't be bluffed, and they object to vacillation with regard to rules. It makes them feel insecure. Therefore, *think* before establishing rules of classroom conduct, and be sure those announced are reasonable and enforceable. Above all, avoid threats!

Every experienced teacher knows what beginning teachers are reluctant to believe; in the beginning it's better to be on the strict side. It's much easier to ease up on control than to tighten it after a loose start. Young teachers are understandably eager to be popular and well liked, but pupils like teachers they respect. In numerous evaluations of student teachers, a comment made again and again by pupils was "I wish he (she) would be more strict with us." Similar comments were "He should make the boys behave," "Why should a few people spoil the entire class," or "I don't like the whole class being yelled at because a few kids misbehave." (Any remark of a remonstratory nature is categorized by adolescents as being "yelled at"; the classification is irrelevant where volume and voice quality are concerned.)

Firmness is important; *fairness* is important. Try to practice both.

Be organized with respect to materials. If confusion reigns when books or papers are being distributed, there is opportunity and temptation for talking, pushing, shoving, and other undesirable "semi-body contact sports" to occur.

Planning for your class is the secret of classroom control. If the class holds the attention of its participants, they will control themselves, of course. Every lesson plan needs some built-in flexibility and on-the-spot changes. But the prepackaged plan is basic. And the packaging should be in terms of *a* plan for *a particular class,* their aptitudes, interests, and experience.

Beginning teachers sometimes operate under an unconscious false assumption: they adopt the college lecture method with their classes. It doesn't work. In fact, it doesn't always work with college classes, as evidenced by open boredom and low attendance in cases of less than expert lecturers. Everything about lecture method in terms of pupil motivation, attention span, and background militates against its effectiveness in junior high school.

With many classes an equally ineffective approach is based on another false assumption. This is the performance-oriented approach, in which the teacher perceives the class as being a quasi-performing unit and proceeds to conduct every class as a miniature rehearsal. The music class is *not* a small chorus. It should not be perceived as a raw material feeder group, but as a class with a defensible instructional purpose in its own right. Rehearse musical organizations, not classes.

If pupils know what the teacher expects of them with regard to behavior, and if the teacher is consistent in staying with stated expectations, pupils are more likely to observe reasonable behavior boundaries. Vacillation from day to day, however, creates unrest and insecurity. Reinforce acceptable behavior—be firm in dealing with unacceptable behavior.

Avoid embarrassing classroom disturbers in front of others. Teachers are adults, and this is all the greater reason for behaving calmly. Sarcasm is a deadly weapon that no youngster can deal with in kind, so it's an unfair one. Pupils will respect a teacher who avoids shows of temper, sarcasm, and other means of "blasting" the class into subservience.

On the other hand, demanding hard, constructive work that makes musical sense may evoke some surface grumbling, but elicits respect and satisfaction where accomplishment is concerned.

Have some easily recognizable signals for routine matters, such as opening classroom procedures. A series of chords on the piano, for example, is better than a shout. And—the teacher should dismiss the class—don't let the class dismiss the teacher!

A sense of humor always helps, especially when the going is rough; try to recognize opportunities to let the class laugh. It's a good energy release and tension reliever.

Beginning teachers should realize that the "let's be pals" approach doesn't seem very real to pupils. *They* know, even if the teacher doesn't, that the role of pal is perceived differently from the teacher role, and that the teacher cannot play both roles effectively. Once a pal, it's difficult to become a teacher again. Be friendly, even in the face of unfriendly pupil attitudes. But keep some distance between you and your pupils. It helps in establishing and maintaining workable rules of conduct.

THE CLASSROOM ATMOSPHERE

Routine matters of classroom management are not the most interesting aspect of music teaching, but concern for them will do much to make teaching more than an endurance contest between teacher and pupils. The classroom can be a pleasant place to work, enjoy music, and learn, or it can be a casual, unplanned room through which pupils pass and spend a restless period or two each week. Here are some suggestions for making it the former:

1. The room temperature is important. It should be approximately 70 degrees; if it goes much higher, the attention of pupils and teacher will dull. Check thermostat and also windows, if you rely on them for ventilation. See that all mechanical arrangements for ventilation are in good working order.

2. Every pupil should be able to *see* and *hear* without straining. Arrange for the best lighting your classroom affords, sometimes combining artificial and natural lighting if necessary.

3. Check your class to make sure that pupils who are handicapped visually, aurally, or otherwise are seated advantageously in relation to handicaps. A little special attention to such matters may mean the difference between success or failure in music.

4. Distribute and collect books and other materials efficiently. Use pupil help but support their efforts with supervision.

5. Junior high school pupils lug many books with them. The youngest often carry so many from class to class that they have difficulty managing them. Let the class know where you expect each book to be left during music class and help them get in the habit of putting books in the assigned place as a matter of routine.

6. When the class needs to use pencil or paper, give them time enough, but not *too* much time, to get out these materials. Most teachers keep a supply of extras on hand—someone always forgets, or loses, his equipment. Is it worth delaying the entire class while he searches or listens to a lecture? Keep it moving!

7. Use bulletin boards for teaching, rather than for announcements. Make them interesting and relevant to class content. See that they are attractive and attention-getting.

8. Use visual *and* aural stimuli thoughtfully. Why not have the record you plan to present playing when the class comes in, with its title on the chalkboard? Or why not be at the piano playing a new or a favorite song as they enter? Even if you believe you should be at the door to dismiss them, you probably don't have to be there to welcome them—but if so, move the piano close to the door and you will be able to do both!

9. *Getting* and *holding* class and individual attention prevent behavior problems and do much to maintain a comfortable classroom atmosphere. Plan for a "stimulator"—an attention-getting device related to the lesson—for beginning the class, and build in a series of subfocal points. Be careful, though, not to overstimulate. Tie stimulators directly to the lesson at hand; use them constructively.

10. If your class will remember only one thing from each lesson, what do you want that one thing to be? Focus your lesson plan!

GOOD TEACHING PROCEDURES

1. Learn pupils' names. If you can address your pupils individually by name, the "Who, me?" reaction won't occur. It is a basic way of letting your pupils know you care about them as individuals.

2. Eye contact with the class is extremely important. Turn the piano, phonographs, and other equipment so you are facing the class when working with the equipment. The teacher's turned back is a temptation.

3. *Practice* placing the needle on the record so that a loud, disturbing noise doesn't result; after all, the class is expecting *music*. The best way to do this is to adjust the volume *before* placing the needle on the record, and again when the needle tracks.

4. Make sure your equipment is in good working order *before* class, not after. Perhaps you can use a mechanically adept pupil as a checker. (There are responsible, knowledgeable pupils who enjoy using their ability helpfully—try to identify them.)

5. Avoid busy-work assignments for classroom or homework.

6. When you make in- or out-of-school assignments, be sure they are relevant, attractive, and of reasonable length. If pupils have a heavy work load of homework, music is not likely to have priority, either with parents or pupils.

7. *Pace* your teaching. Estimate attention span of class; be sensitive to their reactions. Plan for enough variety: singing, listening, working with rhythmic accompaniments. If you are planning to teach a song, for example, bring many musical factors into action to reveal its nature.

8. Plan for a range of individual differences, and keep a quiet check on those who are losing interest because they are ahead of or falling behind the class as a whole. Challenge the accelerated pupils with problem projects they can work on individually; give extra help, but unobtrusively, to the slower learners.

SPECIAL EDUCATION CLASSES: THE EDUCABLE MENTALLY RETARDED

Whatever the handicaps of the pupils in "special education" classes, the sheer impact of the many problems that confront the teacher is likely to be overpowering. And yet it doesn't really take a super-teacher type to devise a plan for constructive action in these classes. It requires an assessment of pupil strengths, as opposed to handicaps. After six or more years in the public schools, special education pupils will have *both* handicaps and strengths to offer in visible form. The obvious fault in the usual approach to these pupils is that teachers are often so tense about getting them under control that methods for accomplishing this are often unintentionally suppressive, and pupil strengths go unidentified. Suppressed human energy tends to explode in overt actions, some of which take the form of problem behavior. With the best of intentions, the teacher thus may compound an already complex problem.

Pupils in special education classes present an array of handicaps that include the mental, the emotional, and sometimes the physical. Often the class includes a much wider age range, too, than the usual class. At first contact with such a class, the teacher would be well advised to collect as much information as possible about its members, using school records as one source, informal pupil interviews as another. With this as a basis, she should set about doing everything possible to make each pupil feel like an individual who possesses both musical potential and personal dignity. Special education pupils differ from others more in degree than otherwise; "average" or "normal" classes also present a wide range of differences. This means that, by and large, the same musical materials may be used, but with different approaches and emphases.

Mentally retarded youngsters hear and enjoy music, respond rhythmically, sing and play instruments. They participate in most of the musical activities their more intelligent peers do. The difference is that they are not as proficient, less able to deal with symbols and abstractions, and usually not as adept in musical manipulation, and they have a shorter attention span.

Use materials that are appropriate to the social maturation age level of the pupils. Do not use elementary level songs with junior high school pupils. Help them feel that they belong to an age group, not that their handicap separates them from it.

Avoid *stress* on abstractions and symbolic involvement with music; deal with its specific and concrete aspects. In presenting the "Cloudburst" section of Grofé's *Grand Canyon Suite,* a teacher wanted the class to understand that the lightning effect was made in part by use of the piano. She showed the class how this was done, then invited them to try it. They also experimented with tympani, creating thunder effects. When they heard the composition, the class had a concrete experiential frame of reference to help them understand and enjoy the music.

In building a repertoire of musical understanding, use musical action even more with these pupils than with those of average intelligence. If, for example, you want them to learn the names of percussion instruments, such as maracas, triangle, or cymbals, demonstrate the instruments and put their names on the chalkboard, then have the students select the *name* of a particular instrument and try playing it. In the process, have pupils select the particular instrument named from a group of instruments, thus relating the word (symbol) to the object. In this way the abstract or symbolic relationship develops more easily.

Mentally retarded pupils enjoy participation in creative activities, making up musical plays, role playing, preparing programs to share with other classes or with parents. They can listen to and report on (give their impressions of) radio and television programs. There are many films and filmstrips that are of value for use in these classes, and the visual aspect of such materials holds interest.

No one can anticipate all the problems that will occur in such classes, but most of the educable retarded can participate in the bulk of musical activities, although emphasis on cognitive aspects must not be the thrust. Avoid tedious language-reading tasks; help with meaning of texts; try not to frustrate pupils with music reading. Eliminate key signature memorization; many youngsters of *average* intelligence don't find such assignments relevant or easy to learn. Be overly patient and understanding, and praise constructive efforts, even if they do not represent high level achievements. Above all, help your pupils succeed in some musical tasks appropriate to their age level, and recognize their achievements. This is important both to their present self-perception and to future goals and aspirations.

7

What Kind of a
Music Teacher
Will You Be?*

THE CHALLENGE OF MUSIC EDUCATION

What kind of a music teacher will you be? The challenge of music education lies in the teacher's ability to help his pupils develop a knowledge of what music means in the lives of human beings; how it can be utilized as a means of self-expression and self-fulfillment; how to understand, evaluate, and use its tremendous force effectively. Note that the teacher's challenge is to *help his pupils develop this*. It is fair to say that the objective, then, is the teacher's ability to communicate his musical knowledge effectively and in such a way that the pupil will be motivated to *propel himself* into increasingly discriminating musical activity and learning. We are discussing here the way people

* This chapter has been adapted from two articles originally published in the *Music Educators Journal*, LIV, No. 2 (October, 1967) pp. 37-38, and Vol. LV, No. 9 (May, 1969), Undergraduate Edition, first two pages. Used by permission.

and music interact and behave when placed together. In other words, music is nothing unless there are people making it, absorbing it, criticizing and evaluating it, and using it in any other ways that seem relevant and important. Music is a communicative art, which means it must have a communicator and a communicatee.

In order to accomplish our goals, we need to ask certain questions: *Who* are the pupils to be taught? *How* do they behave musically without us? Above all, how do we want them to behave musically after we have taught them? Will we have changed their everyday musical behavior, and if so, will we have improved it? Will they be more sensitive and responsive to music? It *is* possible for musical instruction to alienate students, just as it may possibly win them over to a lifelong, constructive association. Frankly, not many music educators stop to ask themselves these questions, and the tendency of too many is to zero in on much mechanical musical or verbal activity.

The challenge of music education is to teach music to children and youth so that their adult lives will be *different* than they would have been without music instruction. They will not be different only from the viewpoint of reminiscing about "What a good time I had when I sang in the high school performance of *The Mikado,*" but from the standpoint of music affecting adult lives in terms of playing and singing; choosing music on radio or television; buying musical equipment such as phonographs, pianos, tape recorders, recordings; and supporting community musical organizations and concerts. In another sense, the desired change is in terms of *changing behavior* so that a sense of joy, exultation, and pleasure, as well as a sense of understanding, is brought into the adult life through the medium of music. This is a real and self-fulfilling change.

If music is to be taught from the standpoint of expecting it to influence the behavior of our pupils, we must discover a great deal about the implications of music as it affects behavior. We know that music can make people happy and sad, that it can alter their physical behavior (for instance, by making them march faster or slower or work more rapidly); we know that music produces feeling in people, although we usually tell children that the music itself has a mood (which is not true, since the mood is in the ear and mind of the beholder).

There is another, almost reverse, angle to this whole problem, that of determining what musical behaviors we want to stimulate. Before we can really do this well, each music educator should try to identify the many diverse ways in which his pupils are already behaving musically. Whereas music education programs tend to view only certain traditional modes of musical behavior as being approved and blessed, there is, in reality, a great diversity of musical behaviors going on around us all the time. Some of these behaviors we see in people playing all kinds of musical instruments—guitars, zithers, various folk instruments, social instruments such as ukulele and the harmonica, and semi-folk instruments such as the accordion. Certain of these instruments are among the most popular in the nation today—for example, the guitar outsells many, many other instruments. In other words, people are behaving musically with the guitar. (No definition of "behaving musically" is needed here, except to note that it implies interaction of an individual with a musical medium.) People are singing, some of them in concert style with highly trained voices, others with such untrained voices that many persons refuse to accept this as even approaching a type of musical behavior. Nevertheless, these individuals are interacting with music in some form or other. People are buying recordings, phonographs, and television sets through which they may or may not consume music, toy trumpets for their children, Auto-harps, and more conventional musical instruments such as violin, trumpet, clarinet. Large groups of pupils in every school system are organized into bands, orchestras, and choruses; they are behaving musically. A child is sitting in his crib humming—this can be considered early evidence of musical behavior.

And in addition to the voluntary interaction of man and music, there is a whole form of imposed musical environment, to which people must submit whether or not they so wish. Music is in planes, busses, terminals, super-markets, dentists' offices; in all such situations we are supplied with music with which to interact. It is true that we may react on a subliminal level, not consciously noting the musical environment. But nevertheless, it is there. All of this affects the teacher of music. He must cope with it, because it is part of his pupils' environment.

Here are some ways in which teachers may use these many musical behaviors, influences, and environmental forces constructively:

1. If your pupils are enthusiastic about any kind of music, don't put it down. Try to recognize its best features, discuss them, and compare them with "better" music that has similar features. For example, some of the country pop tunes are really ballads. Madrigal groups could perform them. Look for such characteristics, and recognize them in your teaching.

2. Any music you and your pupils like has certain similar characteristics. It is all either played or sung, so you can discuss the musical medium. It all has a tempo, faster or slower, andante, lento, or whatever. It is all louder or softer (dynamics); it all utilizes the element of pitch— higher, lower—for melody, harmony, counterpoint. It has some kind of form. You can compare whatever music the pupils "turn on to," using their terms, and you can get them to listen to your kind of music, too. If you think of teaching in terms of games strategy, re-member that while half the moves may be yours, it's very important to pay attention to the pupils' moves. It may require painful honesty

and some rather tortured flexibility to recognize that integration has come to the arts, but the fact is clear. We have a "music mix" in our society, and it is so compelling to a large group of young people that another painful fact is evident—the mainstream of music is moving away from the schools. This mainstream music mix accommodates a wide variety of tastes and is wild, alive, exciting, and tolerant of hybrid forms and sounds. Its contents are "blenderized" in terms of content and style. We also have a mix of music makers; for example, some of the rock musicians have traditional musical educations from outstanding institutions.

3. The emphasis of music history, in terms of literature performed, tends to confine itself to a period of about 300 years. But young people are reaching out for a wider experience with musical styles. Ethnomusicology is a big word today and represents a growing field. Raga to rock, country-rock, soul music—interest in these and more indicates a need for knowledge, feeling, and different sounds. It seems to be a healthy interest. We should transmit our musical heritage concentration of 300 years or so, but extend it and encourage our pupils in a wider variety of musical interests. *Not tolerate—encourage.* And not only *encourage* them; *join them.* Stretch to do it, and you may find your knowledge increasing, as well as your musical influence. But a word of warning: the line of the purists is to advise against such behavior, on the grounds that "it is lowering your standards." It should be pointed out that standards are what society makes them and what teachers are astute enough to help pupils develop. No one ever really aided the development of standards by repudiating existing tastes; such development derives from understanding, acceptance, and growth beyond one particular point to another point that represents achievement of one kind or another. Repudiation by a teacher amounts to suppression; this doesn't work in nondemocratic, let alone democratic, societies. Think in terms of *developing* tastes and standards, rather than *raising* or *lowering* them. Think in terms of using the total musical environment perceptively and discriminatively, rather than ignoring all but a certain part stamped *Approved* by teacher and school.

4. Remember that the pupil who has different ideas from yours isn't necessarily wrong—he's just different. His difference may be his strength. Don't let it be your weakness. The most creative pupils are usually different. Explore their musical ideas; help those ideas work.

What is the challenge of music education? The challenge is for you to be better than any teachers have been in the past, and the opportunity is there. What kind of a teacher will you be?

SOME GUIDEPOSTS FOR BEGINNING TEACHERS

Many of the criteria employed as a basis for judging the work of beginning teachers are routine rather than thought-provoking. Check lists are too often *checked* rather than reflectively considered; subjective comments are sometimes overly influenced by personality factors: both are, of course, extrinsic to the subject of the judgment. The value of some of the standard items that appear on reference forms and teacher rating sheets is questionable. What is needed when a young teacher attempts to assess his own work is a provocative basis for self-reflection.

The following guideposts are intended to serve particularly as a source of evaluation for one major aspect of teaching—the relationship between the teacher and his class, the teacher and his individual pupils. This is the dynamic center, the magnetic pole of the teaching situation, and as such, understanding of the points listed can mean the difference between accepting early teaching experiences with grace and confidence, or despairing because of frustration and misunderstanding.

1. Much confusion and disorganization in music classes and musical organizations results because pupils do not understand what it is they are supposed to be learning. Pupils *must* identify, understand, and accept their goals, whether these are musical or otherwise. Therefore the teacher must identify, understand, and explain the goals set for each music group and class, whether for a period, a term, a class, a rehearsal, or a concert. For example, singing a song should be enjoyable, but since it is a learning activity it should be *purposeful;* learning to play an instrument should be enjoyable, but chiefly a purposeful musical activity—one learns to play an instrument in order to make music. And so it is with any musical activity. Enjoyment is desirable in the learning process, but so is learning.

2. The pupil must know whether or not he has made progress toward reaching the goal set. Any musical experience, whether it be performing a piece of music, participating in a rhythmic activity, or whatever, acquires significance in terms of progress toward a recognized goal and realization of the fact that such progress has been made. The teacher alone can identify such progress and help the pupil recognize it.

3. Every class, every rehearsal, should place emphasis on clearly identified major points. The teacher must determine what such major foci are. In some lessons emphasis may be placed successfully on only one point; in others, on several. For example, in rehearsing a Bach cantata emphasis may be placed on both the importance of phrasing in itself and the importance of phrasing polyphonic music. Whatever these foci or emphases, pupils should recognize and understand their relevance to the musical activity at hand.

4. One of the problems of beginning teachers is that so many pressures beset them in the presence of a class it is easy to regard the class as a *class* rather than as individuals. Perhaps this is because the class as a group can seem less real than an overwhelming complexity of individual entities. But pupils need recognition as individuals. It

cannot be said too often that they need tokens of praise, at least, for correct responses, and more than a "yes" or nod-of-the-head acknowledgment. Such recognition takes a little time but works magic with the teacher-pupil relationship.

5. Pupils in any music class or organization present a staggering inequality in depth and breadth of musical background. The teacher's job is to assess this factor and determine an effective approach to the variety of individuals in the class. We should teach individuals, but we are usually confronted by *classes* of individuals. The teacher is the only equalizing factor available in this situation.

6. Many beginning teachers are overly disturbed by a show of undesirable pupil behavior, which they sometimes regard as a personal affront. It should be understood that manifestations of aggression or other undesirable behavior are not necessarily demonstrations of hostility against the teacher himself. Pupils have their good and bad days, and as immature human beings are easily disturbed by factors bearing little relationship to the classroom or the teacher personally. Placing too much emphasis on transitory behavior may have the undesirable effect of freezing it into a pattern of personal hostility.

7. A host of perplexing problems confronts each beginning teacher. The more sensitive and intelligent he is, the more likely it seems he will be aware of a series of never-ending problems that may at times appear overwhelming. In reality, such problems present an avenue of learning. No one expects the beginning teacher, or even the teacher of many years' experience, to know *everything*. Indeed, it seems possible that the teacher who apparently has few problems may be unaware of some of the real challenges facing him.

8. The music teacher's important task is to teach children music. Related subjects, such as history, mythology, dancing, arithmetic, literature, and art, are avenues for *enrichment* of the teaching of music. When too much time is spent on such activities as relating sundry incidents in the lives of composers rather than playing, singing, hearing, and discussing their music, emphasis is being placed on history and biography, not music. (This comment is not intended to apply to humanities or related arts courses where a team of teachers combine their knowledge of various fields in order to bring a rich core of experiences to pupils.)

9. Few beginning teachers realize that pupils know much more than they can express verbally, than the teacher can ever determine by questioning them. This inability to express ideas is due to a number of factors—to lack of verbal facility, limited vocabulary, and even inability to understand a question as it is phrased. A question that is perfectly clear to the teacher may be cloudy to the pupil. Pupils may make valid responses in their own mode of expression, but because this does not fit the pattern expected by the teacher, they may be scored low. This, of course, is a measure of the teacher's inability to understand as well as the pupil's inability to communicate.

10. The beginning teacher comes into contact with many ideas, methods, and modes of teaching different from those to which he was exposed in his undergraduate classes. The teacher who looks for the best in

each of the many ways he sees teaching being carried on in the schools and thoughtfully examines the desirable and undesirable points of each method is likely to benefit more than the individual who arbitrarily rejects anything new and different from what he was taught. One of the characteristics of a great teacher is his ability to see many different viewpoints and to use constructively elements from many of them. The teacher who rejects anything but a small segment of ideas is arbitrarily limiting his own growth, his horizons, and those of his pupils.

11. The pupils each beginning teacher instructs are living individuals who bring to the classroom a wealth of musical ideas, experiences, and attitudes. This wealth can be used to make the classroom a vital, exciting place in which to discover the magnificent treasures of music *if* the teacher can identify it.

Finally, if only one point could be made that would remain in the teaching technique always, it would be this: Whatever music is used in each class, its preparation should be given the same attention and care as that given to the preparation of a major concert or recital. A simple folk song taught to a class of thirty or forty will be presented to the most impressionable audience in the world—growing, sensitive children. Will it be sung musically, accurately, with a fine voice and understanding of its message and meaning? Will care be taken to spend the time necessary to communicate the music to watching eyes, listening ears, sensitive hearts and minds? Will the recordings used be a means of unlocking the world of music to all pupils, a fine experience in coming closer to the heart of music? Only if they are painstakingly prepared. Music is a hard taskmaster, and what we communicate to our pupils, we must first learn, then *overlearn*. But the willingness and self-discipline necessary to do this are the greatest distinguishing characteristics of the outstanding teacher.

Junior High School
Music Books*

ALLYN & BACON, INC., 470 Atlantic Ave., Boston, Massachusetts 02210

Forcucci, Samuel L., *Let There Be Music*, 1969. Annotated teacher's edition.

McGehee, Thomasine C., *People and Music*, rev. by Alice D. Nelson, 1968.

Sur, William R., Charlotte Dubois, and Robert E. Nye, *This Is Music, Book Seven*, 1968. Teacher's edition; two records.

————, *This Is Music, Book Eight*, 1968. Teacher's edition; two records.

AMERICAN BOOK COMPANY, 300 Pike Street, Cincinnati, Ohio 45202

Berg, Richard C., Daniel S. Hooley, and Josephine Wolverton, *Music for Young Americans*, Book Seven, 1963. Teacher's annotated edition; teacher's guide; Guide and Accompaniment; BM-7 album (2 twelve-inch records).

————, *Music for Young Americans*, Book Eight, 1963. Teacher's annotated edition; teacher's guide; Guide and Accompaniments; BM-8 album (2 twelve-inch records).

* The author acknowledges with thanks the assistance of Mary Lou Romanek in compiling and checking materials listed in this section of the book.

FOLLETT PUBLISHING COMPANY, 1010 West Washington Blvd., Chicago, Illinois 60607

Leonhard, Charles et al., *Discovering Music Together: Elements and Style,* 1970. (Teacher's edition and records available.)

————, *Discovering Music Together: Our Musical Heritage,* 1970. (Teacher's edition and records available.)

————, *Discovering Music Together, Book Seven,* 1966. Teacher's edition; records: albums L700-2, S703-6.

————, *Discovering Music Together, Book Eight,* 1967. Teacher's edition; records: albums L800-2; album L25, *Origins and Development of Jazz.*

Wolfe, Irving et al., *Music Sounds Afar,* 1963. Teacher's edition; 3 records: L71-6.

————, *Proudly We Sing,* 1963. Teacher's edition; 2 records: L81-2.

GINN AND COMPANY, Statler Building, Boston, Massachusetts 02117.

Pitts, Lilla Belle et al., *Singing Juniors,* 1953. Teacher's manual; records: album 7-A, 2 records; album 7-B, 2 records; album 7-C, 1 record.

————, *Singing Teenagers,* 1954. Teacher's manual; records: album 8-1, 2 records; album 8-B, 2 records; album 8-C, 1 record.

————, *Music Makers,* 1956. Album 9, 3 records.

HOLT, RINEHART AND WINSTON, INC., 383 Madison Ave., New York 10017

Landis, Beth, and Lara Hoggard, *Exploring Music, Junior Book,* 1968. Teacher's edition.

————, *Exploring Music, Senior Book,* 1969.

MILLS MUSIC, INC., 250 Maple Ave., Rockville Center, New York 11571

Snyder, Alice M., *Music in Our World,* 1962. Paper, cloth.

WARNER BROS.-SEVEN ARTS MUSIC, 619 West 54th Street, New York, New York 10019

Richardson, Allen L., and Mary E. English, *Living with Music,* Volume I (rev. ed.). New York: M. Witmark & Sons, 1966. Volume I, soft cover, hard cover.

————, *Living with Music,* Volume II (rev. ed.). New York: M. Witmark & Sons, 1958. Volume II, hard cover, soft cover.

PRENTICE-HALL, INC., Englewood Cliffs, New Jersey 07632

Ehret, Walter, Lawrence Barr, and Elizabeth Blair, *Time for Music,* 1959. Teacher's guide, 1960; records: set of 5.

————, *Music for Everyone*, 1959. Teacher's guide, 1960; records: set of 5.

————, *You and Music: Books One and Two*, 1959.

Wilson, Harry R. et al., *Growing with Music, Book Seven*, 1966. Teacher's edition; records.

————, *Growing with Music, Book Eight*, 1966. Teacher's edition; records.

SILVER BURDETT COMPANY, Box 362, Morristown, New Jersey 07960

Cooper, Irvin et al., *Music in Our Life*, 1967. Teacher's edition; records: Set I, 1-4; Set II, 5-8.

————, *Music in Our Times*, 1967. Teacher's edition; records: Set I, 1-4; Set II, 5-8.

————, *Exploring Music, Books One and Two (Skill Books)*, 1969. Books I and II; teacher's edition.

Eisman, Lawrence, Elizabeth Jones, and Raymond Malone, *Making Music Your Own, Book Seven*, 1967. Book Seven; teacher's edition; records.

————, *Making Music Your Own, Book Eight*, 1968. Book Eight; teacher's edition; records.

Serposs, Emile H., and Ira C. Singleton, *Music In Our Heritage*, 1969. Student's book; source book for teaching; records.

SUMMY-BIRCHARD PUBLISHING COMPANY, 1834 Ridge Ave., Evanston, Illinois 60204

Barbour, Harriot, and Warren S. Freeman, *A Story of Music* (rev. ed.), 1958.

Best, Florence, *Music in the Making*, 1960.

Cotton, Marian, and Adelaide Bradburn, *Music Throughout the World* (rev. ed.), 1960.

Ernst, Karl D., Hartley D. Snyder, and Alex H. Zimmerman, *Birchard Music Series, Book Seven*, 1962. Teacher's edition; records.

————, *Birchard Music Series, Book Eight*, 1962. Teacher's edition; records.

Katz, Adele T., and Ruth H. Rowen, *Hearing—Gateway to Music*, 1959.

Resource Readings

I. GENERAL MUSIC CLASS

Andrews, Frances M., and Joseph A. Leeder, *Guiding Junior-High-School Pupils in Music Experiences,* chap. iii, "The General Music Class." Englewood Cliffs, N. J.: Prentice-Hall, Inc., 1953.

Hoffer, Charles R., *Teaching Music in the Secondary Schools,* chap. xiv, "The Junior High School General Music Class." Belmont, Calif.: Wadsworth Publishing Company, Inc., 1964.

Singleton, Ira C., and Simon V. Anderson, *Music in Secondary Schools* (2nd ed.), part 2, "The General Music Class." Boston: Allyn & Bacon, Inc., 1969.

Sur, William R., and Charles F. Schuller, *Music Education for Teen-Agers* (2nd ed.), chap. iii, "The General Music Class." New York: Harper & Row, Publishers, 1966.

II. PLANNING FOR EVERYONE

Andrews, Frances M., and Clara E. Cockerille, *Your School Music Program,* chap. xix, "Evaluating the School's Music Program." Englewood Cliffs, N. J.: Prentice-Hall, Inc., 1958.

Bernabei, Raymond, and Sam Leles, *Behavioral Objectives in Curriculum and Evaluation*. Dubuque, Iowa: Kendall-Hunt Publishing Company, 1970.

Colwell, Richard, *The Evaluation of Music Teaching and Learning*. Englewood Cliffs, N. J.: Prentice-Hall, Inc., 1970.

Devore, Paul W., *Structure and Content Foundations for Curriculum Development*. Washington: National Education Association, 1968.

Eiss, Albert F., and Mary B. Harbeck, *Behavioral Objectives in the Affective Domain*. Washington: National Science Supervisors Association, 1969.

Ernst, Karl D., and Charles L. Gary, eds., *Music in General Education*. Washington: Music Educators National Conference, 1965.

Hughes, William O., *Planning for Junior High School General Music*. Belmont, Calif.: Wadsworth Publishing Company, 1967.

Kibler, Robert J., Larry L. Barker, and David T. Miles, *Behavioral Objectives and Instruction*. Boston: Allyn & Bacon, Inc., 1970.

Krathwohl, David R., Benjamin S. Bloom, and Bertram B. Masia, *Taxonomy of Educational Objectives, Handbook II: Affective Domain*. New York: David McKay Co., Inc., 1964.

Lehman, Paul R., *Tests and Measurements in Music*. Englewood Cliffs, N. J.: Prentice-Hall, Inc., 1968.

Leles, Sam, and Raymond Bernabei, *Writing and Using Behavioral Objectives: A Learning Packet for Teachers, Students, and Administrators*. Tuscaloosa, Alabama: W. B. Drake & Son Printers, Inc., 1969.

Mager, Robert F., *Preparing Instructional Objectives*. Palo Alto: Fearon Publishers, 1962.

Plowman, Paul, *Unit Seven: Behavioral Objectives in Art and Music*. Chicago: Science Research Associates, Inc., 1969.

Sanders, Norris M., *Classroom Questions: What Kinds?* New York: Harper & Row, Publishers, 1966.

Singleton, Ira C., and Simon V. Anderson, *Music in Secondary Schools* (2nd ed.), chap. iv, "The Development of Refined Perception." Boston: Allyn & Bacon, Inc., 1969.

Woodruff, Asahel D., *Basic Concepts of Teaching*. San Francisco: Chandler Publishing Company, 1961.

Woodruff, Asahel D., "Concept Teaching in Music," in *Perspective in Music Education: Source Book III*, ed. Bonnie C. Kowall, pp. 219-23. Washington: Music Educators National Conference, 1966.

III.   SINGING

Andrews, Frances M., and Joseph A. Leeder, *Guiding Junior-High-School Pupils in Music Experiences*, chap. v, "Junior-High School Singers." Englewood Cliffs, N. J.: Prentice-Hall, Inc., 1953.

Cooper, Irvin, and Karl O. Kuersteiner, *Teaching Junior High School Music*, chap. ii, "A Singing Program," and chap. iii, "Voice Classification." Boston: Allyn & Bacon, Inc., 1965.

Hoffer, Charles R., *Teaching Music in the Secondary Schools,* chap. xii, "Singing and Teen-Age Voices." Belmont, Calif.: Wadsworth Publishing Company, Inc., 1964.

Monsour, Sally, and Margaret Perry, *A Junior High School Music Handbook,* chap. iii, "Singing." Englewood Cliffs, N. J.: Prentice-Hall, Inc., 1963. Second edition, 1970.

IV.   LISTENING TO MUSIC

Andrews, Frances M., and Joseph A. Leeder, *Guiding Junior-High-School Pupils in Music Experiences,* chap. vi, "The Listening Experience." Englewood Cliffs, N. J.: Prentice-Hall, Inc., 1953.

Bernstein, Leonard, *The Infinite Variety of Music.* New York: Simon & Schuster, Inc., 1966.

Bernstein, Leonard, *The Joy of Music.* New York: Simon & Schuster, Inc., 1959.

Bernstein, Leonard, *Young People's Concerts for Reading and Listening.* New York: Simon & Schuster, Inc., 1962.

Bond, Dorothy, *Enjoy Music More.* New York: Project Publications, Inc., 1968.

Britten, Benjamin, and Imogen Holst, *The Wonderful World of Music.* Garden City, N. Y.: Garden City Books, 1958.

Cooper, Irvin, and Karl O. Kuersteiner, *Teaching Junior High School Music,* chap. viii, "The Listening Program." Boston: Allyn & Bacon, Inc., 1965.

Hartshorn, William C., "The Role of Listening," in *Basic Concepts in Music Education,* ed. Nelson B. Henry, pp. 261-91. Fifty-seventh Yearbook of the National Society for the Study of Education, Part II. Chicago: The University of Chicago Press, 1958.

Hoffer, Charles R., *The Understanding of Music,* chap. ii, "Listening to Music." Belmont, Calif.: Wadsworth Publishing Company, Inc., 1967.

Machlis, Joseph, *Music: Adventures in Listening.* New York: W. W. Norton & Company, Inc., 1968.

Mininberg, Ian, ed., *Keyboard; Keyboard Jr.* (periodicals). New Haven: Keyboard Jr. Publications, Inc., n.d.

Monsour, Sally, and Margaret Perry, *A Junior High School Music Handbook,* chap. iv, "Music Listening." Englewood Cliffs, N. J.: Prentice-Hall, Inc., 1963. Second edition, 1970.

Siegmeister, Elie, *Invitation to Music.* Irvington-on-Hudson, N. Y.: Harvey House, Inc., 1961.

V.   CREATIVITY

Bruner, Jerome S., "The Conditions of Creativity," in *Contemporary Approaches to Creative Thinking,* ed. Howard E. Gruber, Glenn Terrell, and Michael Wertheimer. Englewood Cliffs, N.J.: Prentice-Hall, Inc., 1962.

Cheyette, Irving, and Herbert Cheyette, *Teaching Music Creatively in the Elementary School.* New York: McGraw-Hill Book Company, 1969.

Ernst, Karl D., ch., "The Nature and Nurture of Creativity," *Documentary Report of the Tanglewood Symposium,* ed. Robert A. Choate. Washington: Music Educators National Conference, 1968.

Getzels, Jacob W., and Philip W. Jackson, *Creativity and Intelligence: Explorations with Gifted Students.* New York: John Wiley & Sons, Inc., 1962.

Ghiselin, Brewster, ed., *The Creative Process.* Berkeley and Los Angeles: University of California Press, 1952.

Kagan, Jerome, ed., *Creativity and Learning.* Boston: Houghton Mifflin Company, 1967.

Kneller, George F., *The Art and Science of Creativity.* New York: Holt, Rinehart and Winston, Inc., 1965.

Matesky, Ralph, "A Study in Children's Creativity," *Perspectives in Music Education: Source Book III,* ed. Bonnie C. Kowall, pp. 229-32. Washington: Music Educators National Conference, 1966.

Michael, William B., ed., *Teaching for Creative Endeavor, Bold New Venture.* Bloomington: Indiana University Press, 1968.

Stark, Charles J., "Creativity: Its Application to the Theory and Practice of Music Teaching," *Perspectives in Music Education: Source Book III,* ed. Bonnie C. Kowall, pp. 223-29. Washington: Music Educators National Conference, 1966.

Stringham, Edwin J., *Listening to Music Creatively* (2nd ed.). Englewood Cliffs, N. J.: Prentice-Hall, Inc., 1959.

Torrance, E. Paul, *Guiding Creative Talent.* Englewood Cliffs, N. J.: Prentice-Hall, Inc., 1962.

VI. CLASSROOM AND PUPIL MANAGEMENT

Coleman, Jack L., Irene L. Schoepfle, and Virginia Templeton, *Music for Exceptional Children.* Evanston, Ill.: Summy-Birchard Company, 1964.

Dunn, Lloyd M., ed., *Exceptional Children in the Schools.* New York: Holt, Rinehart and Winston, Inc., 1963.

Erickson, Marion J., *The Mentally Retarded Child in the Classroom.* New York: The Macmillan Company, 1965.

Carton, Malinda D., *Teaching the Educable Mentally Retarded.* Springfield, Ill.: Charles C. Thomas, Publisher, 1961.

Gingland, David R., and Winifred E. Stiles, *Music Activities for Retarded Children.* Nashville: Abingdon Press, 1965.

Gnagey, William J., *The Psychology of Discipline in the Classroom.* New York: The Macmillan Company, 1968.

Gray, Jenny, *The Teacher's Survival Guide.* Palo Alto: Fearon Publishers, 1967.

Gray, Jenny, *Teaching Without Tears.* Palo Alto: Fearon Publishers, 1968.

Hoffer, Charles R., *Teaching Music in the Secondary Schools,* chap. v, "Guiding Student Behavior." Belmont, Calif.: Wadsworth Publishing Company, 1964.

Howery, Betty I., "Music Therapy for Mentally Retarded Children and Adults," in *Music in Therapy*, ed. E. Thayer Gaston. New York: The Macmillan Company, 1968.

Mager, Robert F., *Developing Attitude Toward Learning*. Palo Alto: Fearon Publishers, 1968.

Oakland, Lloyd, "Discipline Is Desirable!" in *Music Education in Action*, ed. Archie N. Jones, pp. 312-15. Boston: Allyn & Bacon, Inc., 1960.

Robins, Ferris, and Jennet Robins, *Educational Rhythmics for Mentally and Physically Handicapped Children*. New York: Association Press, 1967.

Stenhouse, Lawrence, ed., *Discipline in Schools: A Symposium*. New York: Pergamon Press, Inc., 1967.

Wiener, Daniel N., *Classroom Discipline and Achievement*. Dubuque, Iowa: William C. Brown & Company, 1969. In preparation.

VII. WHAT KIND OF MUSIC TEACHER WILL YOU BE?

Bugelski, B. R., *The Psychology of Learning Applied to Teaching*, chap. xii, "Practical Applications of Psychology to Learning: A Summary." Indianapolis: The Bobbs-Merrill Company, Inc., 1964.

Hoffer, Charles R., *Teaching Music in the Secondary Schools*, chap. iv, "The Complete Music Teacher." Belmont, Calif.: Wadsworth Publishing Company, 1964.

Kaplan, Max, *Foundations and Frontiers of Music Education*, chap. viii, "Music Education as a Profession." New York: Holt, Rinehart and Winston, Inc., 1966.

Leonard, George B., *Education and Ecstasy*, chap. v, "The Rogue as Teacher." New York: Delacorte Press, 1968.

Sur, William R., and Charles F. Schuller, *Music Education for Teen-Agers* (2nd ed.), chap. xiv, "The Teacher and His Responsibilities." New York: Harper & Row, Publishers, 1966.

VIII. GENERAL RESOURCE MATERIALS

Bauer, Marion, and Ethel R. Peyser, *How Music Grew* (rev. ed.). New York: G. P. Putnam's Sons, 1939.

Bauer, Marion, and Ethel R. Peyser, *Music Through the Ages* (3rd ed.), ed. and rev. Elizabeth E. Rogers. New York: G. P. Putnam's Sons, 1967.

Buchanan, Fannie, and Charles L. Luckenbill, *How Man Made Music*. Chicago: Follett Publishing Company, 1959.

Fox, Sidney, *Origins and Development of Jazz* (teacher's ed.). Chicago: Follett Educational Corporation, 1968. Record: Album L25.

Glenn, Neal E., William B. McBride, and George H. Wilson, *Secondary School Music*. Englewood Cliffs, N.J.: Prentice-Hall, Inc., 1970.

Mandell, Muriel, and Robert E. Wood, *Make Your Own Musical Instruments.* New York: Sterling Publishing Company, Inc., 1957.

McKinney, Howard D., *Music and Men.* New York: American Book Company, 1948.

Pleasants, Henry, *Serious Music—and All That Jazz!* New York: Simon & Schuster, Inc., 1969.

Reiner, Bennett, *A Philosophy of Music Education.* Englewood Cliffs, N.J.: Prentice-Hall, Inc., 1970.

Silber, Irvin, *Songs of the Civil War.* New York: Columbia University Press, 1960.

Tanner, Paul, and Maurice Gerow, *The Study of Jazz.* Dubuque, Iowa: William C. Brown, Inc., 1969.

The A-B-C's of Ballet (pamphlet). Greenfield, Mass.: Channing L. Bete Company, Inc., n.d.

The A-B-C's of Symphonies (pamphlet). Greenfield, Mass.: Channing I. Bete Company, Inc., 1954.

Vernazza, Marcelle, *Making and Playing Classroom Instruments.* Palo Alto: Fearon Publishers, Inc., 1959.

SPECIAL ISSUES

"Special Report: Electronic Music," *Music Educators Journal,* LV (November, 1968).

"Special Report: Music in Urban Education," *Music Educators Journal,* LVI (January, 1970).

"Special Report: Youth Music," *Music Educators Journal,* LVI (November, 1969).

Bibliography

A. BOOKS

Andrews, Frances M., "Conceptual Approach to Teaching Music," in *Disciplines Curriculum*, ed. Genevieve Heagney. Towson, Md.: Lida Lee Tall School, Towson State College, 1964. Monograph.

Andrews, Frances M., and Joseph A. Leeder, *Guiding Junior High School Pupils in Music Experiences*. Englewood Cliffs, N. J.: Prentice-Hall, Inc., 1953.

Baldwin, Lillian, *A Listener's Anthology of Music,* Vol. I. Morristown, N. J.: Silver Burdett Company, 1948.

Fleming, William, and Abraham Veinus, *Understanding Music*. New York: Holt, Rinehart and Winston, Inc., 1958.

Mager, Robert F., *Preparing Instructional Objectives*. Palo Alto: Fearon Publishers, 1962.

Russell, David H., *Children's Thinking*. Boston: Ginn and Company, 1956.

B.   PUBLICATIONS OF THE GOVERNMENT, LEARNED SOCIETIES, AND OTHER ORGANIZATIONS

Andrews, Frances M., and Ned C. Deihl, *Development of a Technique for Identifying Elementary School Children's Musical Concepts.* Cooperative Research Project No. 5-0233. Washington: Office of Education, U.S. Department of Health, Education, and Welfare, 1967.

Woodruff, Asahel D., *First Steps in Developing a New School Program* (rev. ed.). Salt Lake City: Bureau of Educational Research, University of Utah, 1968.

Woodruff, Asahel D., and Janyce Taylor, *A Teaching Behavior Code.* M-Step Monograph No. 3. Salt Lake City: Utah State Board of Education, 1968.

Zimmerman, Marilyn Pflederer, and Lee Sechrest, *How Children Conceptually Organize Musical Sounds.* Cooperative Research Project No. 5-0256. Washington: Office of Education, U.S. Department of Health, Education, and Welfare, 1968.

C.   PERIODICALS

Andrews, Frances M. "Guideposts for Beginning Teachers,'" *Music Educators Journal,* LIV (October, 1967), 37-38.

Andrews, Frances M. "What Kind of a Music Teacher Will You Be?" *Music Educators Journal,* LV (May, 1969), Undergraduate Edition.

D.   UNPUBLISHED MATERIALS

Getz, Russell P., "The Influence of Familiarity Through Repetition in Determining Optimum Response of Seventh Grade Children to Certain Types of Serious Music." Unpublished doctoral dissertation, The Pennsylvania State University, 1963.

Laverty, Grace E., "The Development of Children's Concepts of Pitch, Loudness, and Duration as a Function of Grade Level." Unpublished doctoral dissertation, The Pennsylvania State University, 1969.

Woodruff, Asahel D., "Preconference Educational Research Training Project in Music Education, 1969: Blue Papers." Mimeographed.

Index

Index